Leading Teachers

D0496746

Leading Teachers

Helen M. Gunter

continuum
LONDON • NEW YORK

Continuum International Publishing Group
The Tower Building
11 York Road
London
SE1 7NX

15 East 26th Street
New York, NY 10010

www.continuumbooks.com

British Library Cataloguing-in-Publication Data
A catalogue record for this book is available from the British Library.

ISBN: 08264 6456 4 (hardback) 08264 6455 6 (paperback)

Typeset by Fakenham Photosetting Ltd, Fakenham, Norfolk
Printed and bound in Great Britain by CPI Bath

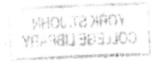

Contents

List of Figures

Series Editors' Foreword

The twin concepts of the last and present decade in education have been those of system transformation and standardization. Across the world, state school systems have been subject to periods of sporadic reform and intervention in the relentless pursuit of school improvement. The global drive for improved educational performance has embraced standardization as the solution to raising standards and improving economic competitiveness. Confronted with demands for better results, standardized solutions certainly offer a low-cost solution for 'a voting public keen on accountability' (Hargreaves 2003, p. 57). In this sense standards-based reform has a 'deceptively simple logic – schools and school systems should be held accountable for their contributions to student learning' (Elmore 2000, p. 4). Responsibility for student learning is located firmly with the school and those who work within it, rather than turning attention to wider social inequities or divisions that contribute to underperformance at system, school and individual level.

Yet, evidence would suggest that while 'soulless standardization' has certainly promoted successive waves of systemic change in many countries, improved educational performance has been much more elusive (Hargreaves 2003). Part of the failure to deliver sustainable improvement in teaching and learning lies in the particular pattern of reform adopted, which is essentially one of increased accountability and restructuring as a route to school improvement. While both these approaches undoubtedly have the potential to promote organizational change, the evidence would suggest that they rarely result in sustainable school and student improvement. Most recently, the RAND evaluation of 'New American Schools' highlights the inadequacies of attempting to reform schools through large-scale, whole-school designs (Berends *et al*. 2002). The evidence here points to the limitations of reform processes where teachers are the recipients rather than the instigators of change. The discourse of education policy in England can be observed to be shifting, with widespread agreement that 'We have reached the high water mark of the post-1997 centrally-driven target-based approach' (Milburn 2004).

Leading Teachers by Helen Gunter is therefore both a welcome and timely book in this series. The title is deliberately ambiguous suggesting that teachers can be expert practitioners as well as being the leaders of change within schools. It is timely because of the recent U-turn in educational policy from competition to collaboration and from individualization to federation. The promise of major educational reform is now firmly located in a local networks and in teachers' ability to transfer knowledge, expertise and good practice, so developing the capacity for sustainable improvement. The epidemic of collaboration is currently sweeping the country in the shape of networked learning communities, partnerships, federations, clusters and consortia. While, in principle, this affords teachers opportunities for greater autonomy from central control and involvement in the process of educational reform, which has to be good, in practice there is a danger that multiple networks can fracture the possibilities for meaningful collaboration between teachers. In short, the structures of collaboration become more important than the processes they are hoping to engender.

Leading Teachers focuses on the processes rather than the mechanics or apparatus of educational reform. It is a book about *educational* leadership, as distinct from the current organizational and outcome-orientated forms of school leadership that are being superimposed on professional practice. Helen Gunter takes the position that teachers need a policy of practice through which they can engage in educational reform, but on their terms and not those dictated by politicians. Her view is that teaching and indeed educational leadership are social practices and therefore teachers are activists through their engagement with what is and what might be.

The book focuses on three key themes: (1) knowledge and knowing about Leading Teachers; (2) the organizational context in which Leading Teachers is located; and (3) knowledge production as the core purpose of Leading Teachers. At the centre of her analysis is the examination of the agency of teachers and ways in which this agency is supported or stifled by organizational structure, culture and politics. As Gunter notes, 'the study and practice of education is about power' and consequently, Leading Teachers presents a major challenge to the existing power structures within schools. For teachers to be leaders implies a reconfiguration of organizational boundaries that enables teachers (and students) to work together in meaningful ways, for example through research. It is a short step to reach the word 'community' or 'communities of practice' to describe the new ways of working, but as Gunter points out, while the trend towards community is a valuable one, without the associated dialogue about power, agency and influence, we are simply replacing one set of organizational parameters for another.

Gunter also highlights the implications for teachers of work intensification and the tensions associated with working in more highly pressurized school environments. Her analysis is realistic rather than pessimistic, suggesting that while 'we cannot change the world overnight, educational leadership requires us to recognize and practise the exercise of power in ways that are productive'. Central to her argument is the need to re-establish trust for, and among, the teaching profession that enables teachers 'to develop their identities and practices through knowledge, knowing and access to a range of knowers'. Her contention is that leading teachers need to embrace their own agency and create opportunities to develop a shared meaning rather than having one imposed upon them.

In her last chapter, Gunter says 'resisting conformity is our greatest challenge'. This is both a motif for this book and a tribute to Helen Gunter's work over many years. This book offers a direct challenge to simplistic notions of leadership that conveniently factor-out social, political and moral considerations. It confronts the aerosol leadership terms based on little empirical substance that colour contemporary thinking about leadership practice. In short, it calls the field to account and asks difficult and provocative questions about who creates knowledge, who has power and who leads. In an educational climate overly receptive to short-term fads and fashions these are important questions which have no automatic answers or instant solutions. For this alone, Helen Gunter's book is worth reading.

Alma Harris
Jane McGregor
Series Editors

References

Berends, M., Bodily, S.J. and Nataraq Kirby, S. (2002) *Facing the Challenges of Whole School Reform: New American Schools after a Decade*, Santa Monica, CA: RAND.

Elmore, R. (2000) *Building a New Structure for School Leadership*, Washington, DC: The Albert Shanker Institute.

Hargreaves, A. (2003) *Teaching in the Knowledge Society*, Maidenhead, Open University Press.

Harris, A. and Lambert, L. (2003) *Building Leadership Capacity for School Improvement,* Buckingham: Open University Press.

Milburn, A. (2004) 'Localism, the Need for a New Settlement', speech at the Design Council, London, available at www.demos.co.uk

Preface

This book is simultaneously familiar and innovative. Much will be known already because it builds on what has gone before (Gunter 1997; 2001), but is challenging because it seeks to look at enduring issues from a different perspective. Familiarity with issues does not necessarily breed contempt, but makes the need for a dynamic education agenda all the more urgent. Questioning should not be read as oppositional but as an example of dialogue and a case for more dialogue. This book is about educational leadership as distinct from the current drive towards organizational and outcome-orientated school leadership. The book is enabling of teachers, but it is not a polemic. The position I take is that teachers need a politics of practice through which they can ask more of themselves than how best to implement reform, and to do more about their situation through the exercise of professional courage in ways that are social and socializing.

This book has been written during a period of study leave from the School of Education at Birmingham, and I am grateful to colleagues for the space to work through the ideas that the book records. During the autumn of 2003 there have been three things that have shaped my thinking and strengthened my resolve in these endeavours. First, there is an increasing recognition that the issues I first raised in 1997 using the metaphor of jurassic management are still with us, and indeed increasingly so (Gunter 1997). If I was to write this book today I would retain the analogy of the theme park as the process and goal of current policy strategies, but I would probably call it Teletubbies' Management. Not to be disparaging to this wonderful programme, but to highlight that the emphasis on integrating the cognitive and affective aspects of being human into the organization as conceptualized by a disembodied adult all-knowing voice distant from practice is creating a way of being in the world that is not only immature for teachers and students but also dangerous for the purposes of schools and schooling. I am going to argue for educational leadership as distributed practice that is relational, and this has implications for how we engage with the school as a public institution. This is underpinned by the need to communicate authentically about who we are and work on how we want to learn together without becoming trapped into totalizing sameness.

A second source of perspective has been generated by the publication of James Gleick's biography of Isaac Newton (2003), in which he shows the interplay between the life and work of Newton, and how that work has over time become Newtonian. His work and the interpretation of his work has structured our world regarding the assumptions we make about what is known and how it can be known. Yet his experiments in alchemy show the enduring tensions between facts and values, science and magic, outcome and process. I am going to continue to argue that educational leadership is an ongoing struggle between the desire for rationality with the reality of a dynamic and pluralistic field, and that what we know, can know and is worth knowing about educational leadership is what we are working for within a structuring context rather than the production of cause-and-effect behaviours and attributes.

The Hutton inquiry into the circumstances surrounding the death of Dr David Kelly provides the third reflexive opportunity for all of us who work in the public sector. At the time of writing the report is not yet published, but what has emerged is the issue of how a public servant felt about his work and his passion for that work. I am going to argue that we need to care about and for our public workers, not in a mushy sentimental way but to enable teachers to know that they matter and that they are valued. Educational leadership depends on teachers knowing and wanting to know more about their practice and their engagement with students and their learning. It needs to be sustained by a public culture that is challenging and demanding but not undermining or ridiculing of teachers.

I am deeply indebted to the range of colleagues from across the education system who are members of the higher degree programmes at Birmingham and who stimulate thinking and open up the possibilities for learning. In particular, I am very grateful to the teachers who have given me access to their work and thoughts that are included in Chapter 4. I am always impressed by their commitment and enduring optimism within new hard times.

Life and work would have been impossible without the insights and labours of a range of people who I am privileged to know and work with. My collaboration with Professor Peter Ribbins in mapping the field has been very fruitful. Our conversations and writing have been a joy, and this book has grown out of and been enabled through this work.

This book is dedicated to the Pathfinder Team in the School of Education who through their endeavours and insights have made a huge and long-term investment into knowledge and knowing by teachers.

Helen M. Gunter
December 2003

1 Leading Teachers

In the election campaign in June 2001 the *Guardian* ran a competition entitled: 'The School I'd Like', and from the 15,000 entries *The Children's Manifesto* was produced:

The school we would like is:
- A beautiful school with glass dome roofs to let in the light, uncluttered classrooms and brightly coloured walls.
- A comfortable school with sofas and beanbags, cushions on the floors, tables that don't scrape our knees, blinds that keep out the sun, and quiet rooms where we can chill out.
- A safe school with swipe cards for the school gate, anti-bully alarms, first-aid classes, and someone to talk to about our problems.
- A listening school with children on the governing body, class representatives and the chance to vote for teachers.
- A flexible school without rigid timetables or exams, without compulsory homework, without a one-size-fits-all curriculum, so we can follow our own interests and spend more time on what we enjoy.
- A relevant school where we are not treated as empty vessels to be filled with information, where teachers treat us as individuals, where children and adults can talk freely to each other, and our opinion matters.
- A school without walls so we can go outside and learn, with animals to look after and wild gardens to explore.
- A school for everybody with boys and girls from all backgrounds and abilities, with no grading, so we don't compete against each other, but just do our best.

At the school we'd like, we'd have:
- Enough pencils and books for each child.
- Laptops so we could continue our work outside and at home.
- Drinking water in every classroom, and fountains of soft drinks in the playground.
- School uniforms of trainers, baseball caps and fleece tracksuits for boys and girls.
- Clean toilets that lock, with paper and soap, and flushes not chains.
- Fast-food school dinners and no dinner ladies.

- Large lockers to store our things.
- A swimming pool.

This is what we'd like.

It is not an impossible dream (Birkett 2001, p. 3).

Such requests are not unreasonable. Learners in all sites of education would likely want much of this, and we can recognize that many of these things are evident right now in some schools. All of it is possible, is consistent with democratic beliefs, and much of it is backed up with research evidence. However, the very people that children and adult learners would need to help them create this type of learning environment are in crisis:

Specialist business

I am 42 years old. I usually work a minimum of 60 hours a week. I manage nearly 50 staff and more than 700 specific clients, who bring well over £1m into my company each year. I also have primary responsibility for capital assets with a value considerably in excess of £3m. I influence corporate strategic policy through regular presentations to the directorate, produce business plans and financial projections, devise and implement marketing and promotional strategies, evaluate new resources and continually create new products to add to the company portfolio.

In the last four years, I have taken roughly 30 days holiday in total. I'm not including those days when I was called in, for example, to urgent meetings, crises such as burglaries or staff sick leave cover, nor the one memorable occasion when I booked five days leave so that I could spend a week undisturbed in my office catching up with paperwork.

Believe it or not, my company is extremely well managed, but most of my colleagues work in similar conditions, and usually for less pay than me. I earn slightly over £26,000 a year, which is good money by most standards, but doesn't, in my opinion, reflect my responsibility for workload. So what's my job?

Here are some clues: my 'clients' are students, my 'products' are degree courses and my 'company' is a college. That's right, I'm a teacher. Head of department, actually, so the duties listed above are in addition to my full-time teaching role. And that's why I'm looking for another job. (Name and address supplied [Anonymous, 4 June 2001])

Research shows that this person is not alone. Thomas *et al.* (2003) identify that the causes of excessive workload are activities that distract from teaching, such as form filling. There is a lack of time in the working day resulting in work being taken home for the evening, weekend and holidays. Teachers in primary schools are working 53 hours per week, in secondary and special schools 51 hours per week. Over 90 per cent of teachers report that they work in the evening and at weekends. Woodward (2003, p. 1) reporting on a General Teaching Council (GTC)/ *Guardian*/Mori survey states that 'one in three teachers expects to leave the profession within five years, protesting about workload, government interference and poor pupil behaviour'. Horne (2001, p. 15) reports on the Ofsted (Office for Standards in Education) estimate that '40 per cent of new teachers leave teaching altogether within three years of entering, while half are expected to quit within five years. Around 300,000 quali- fied teachers are not practising.' When we combine this with reports of a funding crisis and redundancies (Stewart 2003a) then it is highly unlikely that the children's voices underpinning the type of school that they would like will be heard. Where does this leave us? A vital question, given that learners are in schools, colleges and universities right now and those responsible for enabling learning are doing their job and handling dif- ficult choices well. I argue in this book that we are being prevented from working for the type of learning that both teachers and learners want because educational leadership is being marginalized.

Labels and labelling

The title of this book is deliberately ambiguous. One reading is that which is consistent with the current model of school leadership in which teachers are led by others both organizationally through role incumbents such as the headteacher and middle managers, and systemically by those in central government (No. 10 and the Department for Education and Skills [DfES]) and its policy agencies (e.g. the National College for School Leadership [NCSL]) who lead on how schools should be led. In New Labour-speak teachers are 'frontline staff' (Hoggart 2001 p. 14), and the teacher is posi- tioned as an individual who is a member of the school workforce and is in receipt of work delegated to and within the school. This can be a formal division of labour through job descriptions, organizational structures and remuneration agreements, and can be informal with the acceptance of developmental opportunities where additional work is taken on. In this sense distributed leadership is organizational and contractual, and teacher leadership models that of the headteacher in which they are authorized to lead in the middle on organizational matters regarding the purposes and practices of teaching and learning. Hence Leading Teachers is where the teacher is led and only leads others according to organizational and official policy requirements. It is leadership through performativity, based on the teacher as an enthusiastic and committed follower who teaches in accordance with prescribed methods and who uses resources approved and determined by others. The teacher is a flexible worker who can be directed to meet all learning needs and/or be trained to respond to those needs.

New Labour has invested heavily in this approach to leadership, and it is currently being labelled school leadership and promoted by the NCSL as the agency entrusted with its conceptualization and delivery:

> The emphasis on transformation is both deliberate and necessary. Reform strategies and leadership programmes can no longer take only an incremental approach to change to student learning and attainment. This is particularly the case given the ambitious national agenda for sustainable improvement for all students in all settings. Leadership now needs to be seen within a whole school or systems context and to impact both on classroom practice and the work culture of the school. Hence the emphasis on transformation. This implies an expansion in the capacity of the school to manage change in the pursuit of student learning and achievement, and the creation of professional learning communities within the school to support the work of teachers. (Hopkins 2001, p. 8)

The starting point remains that of transformational leadership that has been borrowed from the private sector and used to enable headteachers to have the skills and commitment to deliver government policy (Gunter 2001). The hierarchical dominance of the headteacher role has been sustained through a makeover as a charismatic leader with a vision and a mission for the school. However, recognition that the super-leader accountable for government policy at local level is a likely factor in the headteacher recruitment crisis has led to the development of a hybrid model. For example, the NCSL's model is based on ten propositions. It is stated that school leadership *must*:

- be purposeful, inclusive and values driven;
- embrace the distinctive and inclusive context of the school;
- promote an active view of learning;
- be instructionally focused;
- be a function that is distributed throughout the school;
- build capacity by developing the school as a learning community;
- be futures oriented and strategically driven;
- be developed through experiential and innovative methodologies;
- be served by a support and policy context that is coherent and implementation driven; and
- be supported by a national college that leads the discourse around leadership for learning. (Hopkins 2001, p. 5)

School leadership is based on (1) a separation of organizational leaders from teachers; (2) it is what post holders do and through distribution can take on more responsibility for delivery; (3) it is easily trainable; (4) it is organizational leadership set within a school that disconnects those who work and learn in a school from other educational sites; and, (5) knowledge production is controlled and disseminated by a government agency. While the propositions talk about the focus on learning, the construction of school leadership remains contingent upon learners rather than integral to learning. Learners cannot lead except within the confines of the structures and cultures that have been determined by others. Teachers have organizational functions and required behaviours distributed to them by school leaders, and their leadership of learning cannot have interests or connect with sources of power that question the unity and goal orientation of the school.

This model is the subject of critical evaluation, and the field has been asked to think about some important matters regarding the realities of practice (see Gronn 2003a,b,c). Barnett and McCormick (2003) are cautious, but do challenge whether transformational vision impacts on what teachers actually do, and in drawing on the work of Meindl, they note that 'people tend to exaggerate the effects of leadership because they have implicit theories about organizations, to which they attribute the powerful effects of leadership' (p. 69). Gronn (2003b) has analysed practitioner accounts of their work to show that the binary divide between leading and managing does not exist in the realities of practice, and it is unhelpful to that practice and how we understand and develop that practice. He goes on to argue that the separation of the leader from the follower is through 'designer leadership' and one important effect of this is:

> to standardise experience within those activity realms by eliminating variations in the conduct of practice. The result is that standards can be characterised as solutions in search of problems, in that they prescribe anticipated, legitimated and programmed responses to societal and organisational possibilities yet to be realised. (Gronn 2003b, pp. 9–10)

The consequence, he argues, is that 'growing accountability expectations of school principals and senior teachers to perform as 'super leaders', coupled with the reality of work intensification associated with their dramatically expanded roles, are fuelling a culture of disengagement from leadership among teachers' (Gronn 2003c, p. 29).

We are in danger of losing sight of educational leadership. Educational leadership focuses on the education system, is about education, it is integral to learning processes and outcomes, and it is educative. It is underpinned by a richness of research and theory located in the social sciences, and based on valuing dialogue and differences of views. Hence knowledge claims are concerned with the interplay between the realities of activity and action with working for social and socialized learning. Educational leadership is a social practice and is less about the 'must' of being a leader and more about the meaning and activity of doing leading and experiencing leadership. So educational leadership is concerned with productive social and socializing relationships where the approach is not so much about controlling relationships through team processes but more about how the agent is connected with others in their own and others' learning. Hence it is inclusive of all, and integrated within teaching and learning. While there are formal organizational leaders who have a role and a job description, they are not the only leaders. Students are leaders of their own and others' learning, teachers are leaders of learning both inside and outside the organization. We are able to make our experiences and aspirations for our own and others learning visible. The organization of the school is a public space where democratic structures and cultures, and the necessary practices associated with these, are developed and used. Hence educational leadership is not just the must of delivering efficient and effective organizations but is also about challenging the power structures and cultures that we inherit and that can act as barriers to democratic development.

We can gain perspective on this and develop strategies for action through the intellectual resources that are available from the social sciences. Theorizing about power means that we can examine policy not as a given but as a process that can be inclusive of all through our practice as policy-makers in classrooms, staffrooms and community centres. We can be enabled by our own knowledge and knowing and can have that challenged and developed through our own work as researching professionals in our own and other settings, and by the work of professional researchers undertaken in universities. Our sense of self and identity, both as individuals and within communities, can also be recognized and respected through historical and developmental analyses. Educational leadership is therefore political and as such can be undermined by bad behaviour and self-interest, but not inevitably so. Such activity will also challenge school leadership, but the difference is that those who work for educational leadership give recognition to politics and the realities of humanity, and seek to understand and work within it. We cannot depoliticize human associations and organizations through the adoption of an optimistic generic process, but we can seek to understand through research and theorizing how we might work and live together better.

The second and preferred reading of the book title does not deny the importance of organizational and systemic contractualism, but acknowledges that there are ways of leading and approaches to leadership that enable teachers to lead on their own terms. Hence teachers are leaders through their relationships with each other and with the school and wider publics that they work and associate with. Teachers are leaders in their classrooms, they do leading, and they engage in leadership relationships. They are within and do educational leadership. Hence this book is not about teacher leadership through the tagging on of leadership as a fashionable logo to make the job of higher status. This book is about recognizing that educational leadership has always been a part of being a teacher and doing teacherly things. It may not always have been done well or in the interests of those it is meant to serve, but it is central to how we might begin to engage in a dialogue that will enable teachers and teaching to recapture vitality and validity.

A public life?

Teachers are real people. We breathe, taste, hear, see, smell and talk. We bleed, cry, vomit and laugh. We get it right and we get it wrong, and all places in between. We garden, we worship, we protest, we shop, we paint, we read, we eat. We live a quiet life and we are the national news. We become ill, we recover, we die. We orgasm, we give birth, we are infertile. We have interests and are interesting people. I find it necessary to say these things because much of what is written and said about teachers does not begin with the realities of humanity. It neither acknowledges that teachers are people who do a job of work, i.e. teaching, nor does it recognize that those who are qualified to teach and are experienced in teaching are varied and various in who they are, their values and their beliefs. Like everyone else who walks this earth, teachers are fallible, and like everyone else they have the capacity to handle this through training and professional learning.

There are 438,400 serving teachers in England (DfES 2003a), and their capacity to exercise agency is structured through their gender, age, sexuality, ethnicity and class. Furthermore, dispositions towards knowledge, knowing and knowers within the educational process will have been revealed to individuals either dramatically through a decision to teach mathematics rather than English literature, or incrementally through how the craft of teaching develops over time. Hence we have a highly pluralistic workforce, and so it is difficult to make generalizations, and while we may personally have positive memories of individual teachers it is possible that we also accept the common parlance of teachers as an easily identifiable and coherent group who can be conveniently scape-goated, particularly the media trend to treat teachers as the enemy of good parenting and a waste of taxpayers' money.

Teachers live a public life with all the negativities that this brings and little of the capital gains that others in this setting currently receive in material or symbolic ways. This public life is fourfold: first, teachers do their work in public; second, they are paid from the public purse; third, they contribute to the public good; and fourth, they are members of the public. The public nature of teaching is located in the web of relation-ships that are brought into and extended through classroom activities. Teachers have always been publicly accountable through children's loca-tion at the centre of learning, and how the teacher can become another member of the family (welcome or unwelcome) through discussions and silences about day-to-day highs and lows. A teacher can be simultane-ously hated and respected, permanently or fleetingly, in households and at school gates across the nation. All have been to school, and so all know about teachers and teaching. This knowledge and knowing is structured by wider debates about the efficiency and effectiveness of the public sector, and it is this aspect that can be critical of and critical to teachers.

We are witnessing, and are part of, the ongoing struggle for public education, and we cannot separate out attitudes, beliefs and opinions of teachers and teachers, schools and schooling from that. Public education in England is recent and it has never been secure. At its best public educa-tion is concerned with access and the development of skills with a love of learning, but at its worst it is about selection and training as a means of preparing the child for a preordained place in the world. The failure to invest in both the intellectual and secular infrastructure of education in the second half of the twentieth century meant that the public purposes of schools and schooling and the places where schooling happens have been in decay. As a culture we give little time to ideas, and we have allowed the civic aspect of family life to be othered as irrelevant to our individual interests. Hence we have not invested enough, either politically or eco-nomically, in the social, and teachers and teaching have been the victims of this. We have sought out the shopping mall, the holiday resort and the health club, but we have not sustained a pride in the civic as experiences, buildings or as workers. While the private sector has struggled to come up with a theory of motivation that can predict and sustain productivity, it has never been able to match and sustain the commitment of teachers who engage with immediacy and work until the job is done.

Teachers from the 1960s to the late 1980s, who are a product of the civic (access through the comprehensive school and investment through social security and grants for study in higher education) either continue to work for public-sector values, or comply (wholeheartedly or strategically) with the values of self-interest and protection. Teachers from the 1980s onwards, who are a product of the material (exclusivity in the logoized organization within a quasi-market), have experienced mainly private-sector values and as flexible workers can relocate as and when. When you have a teaching community which doesn't feel safe in its work, and when decisions on knowledge and know how are made at a distance from the classroom by those who don't have to teach or work directly with learners, then teachers will respond accordingly. Some are compliant because they have a mortgage to pay; some are enthused; some take refuge in being awkward. Some leave. Most work very hard to ensure that pupil learning is not too damaged by the latest initiative that is imposed on education or an individual school. Teachers are very good at making things work in adverse conditions. They can achieve high educational standards without the right books, equipment, paper or staffing. They keep returning to classrooms where they have negative experiences with some children; it takes a lot for a teacher to give up on a child. What is central here is how and why teachers do things they don't always or fully believe in. Teachers will face paperwork that they cannot see the relevance of for learning. They will be in receipt of an electronic whiteboard and training for whole-class teaching, but have a class of such varying ages and abilities that makes whole-class teaching inappropriate. They will have to test children at times when those children are not ready to be tested. They will have to transmit content at the expense of learning. They will have to train skills at the expense of content. They will have to tick boxes to show that they have done it. They will have to deny access to learning because teachers who have left have not been replaced due to budget cuts. When they get fed up they can become blockers and staff room cynics: alienated losers who hide enthusiasm and interest through fear of being let down, again. Hence, it seems, teachers who have been put in this situation have to be led out of it through inspirational and charismatic organizational role incumbents.

The challenge of teachers and teaching embraces all of us. Not least because how teachers are positioned by others (parent, business-owner, taxpayer) and how teachers may react to this (arrogance, compliance, resignation) is a result of what Sennett (1999, p. 11) describes as a 'corrosion of character'. This is being experienced across our society and so those who do the positioning (of self and of others) are doing so because they work in 'a regime which provides human beings no deep reasons to care about one another' (p. 148). Consequently, when reasons for teachers leaving the profession are published in the media then they are being read and listened to by people who because of their work context may not respect the argument or those who are making it. The modernized workplace (be it in the private or public sector) does not enable 'people to form their characters into sustained narratives' (p. 31), and so our capacity to create meaningful identities is lost. By telling the story of the impact of computerization in a bakery, Sennett (1999) is able to show the disconnection between people and work:

> It is, I came to realize, the very user-friendliness of the bakery that may account in part for the confusion the people baking feel about themselves as bakers. In all forms of work, from sculpting to serving meals, people identify with tasks which challenge them, tasks which are difficult. But in this flexible workplace, with its polyglot workers coming and going irregu-larly, radically different orders coming in each day, the machinery is the only real standard of order, and so have to be easy for anyone, no matter who, to operate. Difficulty is counterproductive in a flexible regime. By a terrible paradox, when we diminish difficulty and resistance, we create the very conditions for uncritical and indifferent activity on the part of the users ...
>
> The detachment and confusion I found among the bakers in Boston is a response to these peculiar properties of computer use in a flexible work-place. It wouldn't be news to any of these men and women that resistance and difficulty are important sources of mental stimulation, that when we struggle to know something, we know it well. But these truths have no home. Difficulty and flexibility are contraries in the bakery's ordinary productive process. At moments of breakdown, the bakers suddenly found themselves shut out from dealing with their work – and this rebounded to their sense of working self. When the woman in the bakery says 'Baking, shoemaking, printing, you name it', her feel for the machine is of an easy, friendly sort. But she is also, as she repeated to me several times, no baker. These two statements are intimately linked. Her understanding of work is superficial; her identity as a worker is light. (pp. 72–4)

Teaching is being made teacher-proof through centralized curriculum and testing, and through organizational monitoring. In a world of ring-binders and integrated learning packages intellectual work and the emotional interconnectivity with craft knowledge is not needed. While hierarchy and 'the boss' lacks appeal and appropriateness to our working lives in education it is being replaced by team work which 'is the group practice of demeaning superficiality' (Sennett 1999, p. 99). Teachers and learners are given ways of working that are presented as safe and productive but continue to be about the exercise of power in which they are made to be responsible but have little authority. There is a sense in which we all know each other because there are lists of what effective teachers do, and those appointed to enact this have been trained and licensed, and so are fit for the purpose. However, what we are not allowed to do is to confront 'the strange and unknown' (Sennett 2002, p. 19) because the content of what we are allowed to do is scripted by those at a distance from us, and the skills we need to do it are easily trainable. We can be made to feel good about this because the language and process of team-working is an example of 'intimate tyrannies' where we are seduced into 'one standard of truth to measure the complexities of social reality' (Sennett 2002, pp. 337–8). Teams are places where the organization matters more than the social; where consensus matters more than ideas; where celebrity matters more than integrity; and where delivery matters more than dialogue. As Sennett (2002) argues, we witness the unfairness of class, gender, ethnicity in our everyday lives, but we do not necessarily translate this knowing into productive political activity, and so while the rhetoric of transformation is endemic, little actually changes.

Who knows?

Teachers are knowers about learning, they do knowing through what they do, and use and produce knowledge about what they do. Desforges

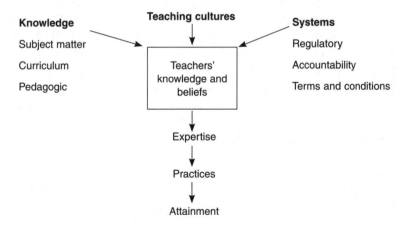

Figure 1.1 Forces shaping practice
Source: Desforges 2003, p. 6.

(2003) presents a way of understanding what teachers do as practice and this is shown in Figure 1.1.

The diagram is based on two main assertions: 'teachers' practices are shaped by their knowledge, attitudes and beliefs' (p. 6) and 'pupils are directly influenced only by their teachers' practices' (p. 7). Desforges argues that the diagram should be read from the bottom up, and so we should begin with attainment as the outcome of teachers' practice as 'teaching in action' (p. 7). He goes on to argue that

> Expertise refers to the teachers' wisdom and judgement in making specific decisions at all stages of the teaching process, i.e. in the planning, inter-action and evaluation phases. Expertise mediates between the teachers' knowledge and belief systems and the reading of the situation to hand. Expertise is an interpretative process drawing in part on a corpus of formal and tacit knowledge. In regard to teaching subject matter, teachers have an extensive grasp of the academic material *per se*. In addition, they have knowledge of a wide range of ways and means by which the subject is represented in curriculum materials. Teachers also hold a body of related pedagogic knowledge which refers to, for example, those concepts which are difficult to learn, or those methods of relating pupils' current know-ledge to available curriculum representations. (Desforges 2003, p. 7)

This practice does not happen in a vacuum, but is located in networks in school and beyond, and is structured by their understanding of pro-fessional cultures and systemic regulations. Evidence about the impact of teacher interventions to produce learning is in abundance: first, in classrooms through ongoing feedback (listening, looking, questioning) and reflection with action research providing a structured way in which enquiry can generate research data to be used to support development; and, second, in schools through attainment data at the end of key stages. However, what is of concern is how research undertaken by others and in different settings could be used by teachers to develop their practice. Evidence-informed practice is the means by which this can take place, so that when decisions are made about pupil grouping, or questioning, or a learning activity, it is based on what is known about good practice. Teachers can access this through web-based provision of research findings constructed from systematic reviews of the literature. It is reasoned that if teachers gather and use data in their classrooms to monitor learning then their interpretation of this data has to be connected to research about how best to improve learning opportunities.

One way of handling this has been to critique educational researchers for failing to do research that is of relevance to the teacher in their practice, for disseminating it in ways that are elitist and for excluding the teacher as user of evidence from the research process. This has either been through an all-out attack on educational researchers or by adopting systematic reviews of the literature that privileges particular knowledge claims and ways of working (Ribbins and Gunter 2003). The response has been varied, but there have been productive replies and debates (Hammersley 2001) and accounts about participation in systematic reviews (Bell *et al.* 2003). An alternative, but not unconnected, approach has been to focus on the nature of teaching and learning, and how evidence is and could be used. Desforges (2003) examination of teacher practice therefore provides us with an opportunity to engage with this and to examine what it means to use evidence, and he shows the problematics of rational argument and how we respond to challenges to how we see and understand the world. We can be conservative, and downright awkward, and it seems that we only yield and change our ways when the evidence is overwhelming. Hence, 'evidence-informed practice will take a lot more than evidence' (p. 9), and given that we are seeking to change practice that is human rather than technological then 'the development of evidence-informed practice ... is more likely to be achieved through manipulation of the inspection regime and through statutory measures than through processes of persuasion, or professional development based on professional responsibilities' (p. 10). This is a very depressing scenario. The inspection regime and educational reform have not always treated teachers or their work with respect, and much of what teachers are directed to do is not based on evidence that teachers or researchers trust; moreover, it is presented in ways that tend to undermine dialogue.

Desforges' model represents the teacher as a powerful person to deliver attainment, and hence enables the teacher to be the focus of reform. I would want to develop Desforges' model through a sociological approach to *developing learning*, where we can engage with the student in relationship with others who are there to support, enable and direct that learning. Those others are primarily teachers, but also include students and members of the school workforce, such as teaching assistants, the bursar and site manager, who directly and indirectly assist students and teachers in classrooms. This is not to let teachers off the hook, but to recognize that activity in schools is too vast and specialized for them to do it alone. Furthermore, the purposes of developing learning are not just attainment. This is important in regard to credentials, but we must also recognize achievement as being about a disposition for learning that may not be directly measurable at legislated times. The wider purposes of schools and schooling are places where we develop and challenge our identity regarding who we are and what we do, and this is essential to an authentic and mature democratic citizenship.

Developing learning is an ongoing productive struggle in which students and teachers are both knowers about teaching and learning. Students bring to this relationship who they are (gender, class, ethnicity, religion, politics) and have expectations of themselves and others regarding the compulsory setting in which they are located. As students spend less than 20 per cent of their time in formal schooling then we have to acknowledge that learning in other contexts will be brought into the classroom in ways that may or may not support teachers' practices. As teachers are real people with wider lives then they too not only bring into school the teaching, cultural and systemic knowledge, as defined by Desforges, but also their professionality in their capacity to be social and socializing people. Structures simultaneously limit and enhance teacher agency, and in order to understand this we need to be working for an understanding that is deeper and richer than that provided by mere formal evidence. In making decisions with students about their learning, teachers need to engage in conceptually informed practice (Gunter 2001). Such work is intellectual work; it is challenging; it begins with teachers as knowers who have a legitimate right to reject knowledge not because they are necessarily conservative or self-serving but because they know. Teachers need professional development to access their knowing, to challenge this knowing, and to develop new ways of knowing. Teaching is a social practice that is active, and as such teachers are activists in their engagement with was is and what might be.

A working dialogue

In working for educational leadership I intend to continue the dialogue by focusing on three key themes in the book: (1) knowledge and knowing about Leading Teachers; (2) the organizational context in which Leading Teachers is structured; (3) knowledge production as the core purpose of Leading Teachers. At the heart of my analysis is an examination of the agency of teachers to control their practice and how that agency is enhanced and stifled by structures such as the organization. In Chapter 2 I intend to use an approach to charting knowledge production in order to examine the growth in teacher leadership and to open up other areas of knowledge and knowing together with the knowers so that the full dynamics of agency and assumptions about agency within field activity are revealed. In Chapter 3 I focus on structure, and in particular organizational structures, that impact on teachers and their work. I draw on theories of power to examine the current debates about distributed leadership. In Chapters 4 and 5 I move on to examine the interplay between agency and structure in relation to research practice. The emphasis is on examining conceptually informed practice and how intellectual work is relevant to teacher work and identity. Chapter 6 draws together the case for educational leadership as being worth working for through and with Leading Teachers. I raise the implications of this for students and role incumbents, and so present an agenda for taking the dialogue forward.

2 Dimensions of Leading Teachers

If we are to engage in the praxis of Leading Teachers then we need to have a description and understanding of the knowledge claims within the field. In this chapter I intend looking at different positions in the knowledge production process with a view to making visible the pluralistic nature of the field: its dimensions and its possibilities. This analysis will be shaped by my collaborative work with Peter Ribbins on mapping the field and how we seek to understand and give recognition to knowledge claims (Gunter and Ribbins 2003a,b). Consequently, I am presenting myself as a mapper, I am doing mapping and this chapter (and indeed the book as a whole) is a map. I bring to this process my experience of being a leading teacher and doing leadership. In doing mapping I intend to draw on a range of intellectual resources and produce an account, with the map as a construction that should be critically engaged with. This chapter is not an empty narrative, but is the product of and a contribution to conceptually informed practice. As such, I do not approach my reading and my position on that reading as 'ritual embalming' (Bourdieu 2000 p. 48) through which ideas form a canon that is worshipped and replicated. Intellectual work requires critical evaluation that is not inevitably oppositional but is about identifying and opening up spaces for ways of understanding the world that affirm our practice and our challenge to that practice.

The growth of what is known as 'teacher leadership' is acknowledged by Harris (2003) to be a significant part of the field in the USA and Canada, but has only recently begun to feature in England. She goes on to argue that

> Teacher leadership is either dismissed as yet another label for continuing professional development or simply rejected because of the complexities of viewing teachers as leaders within a hierarchical school system where leadership responsibilities are very clearly delineated. The fact that schools rely on a clear demarcation of roles and responsibilities presents a major barrier to the idea of teachers as leaders. (p. 314)

Nevertheless, Harris shows that there are possibilities for other ways in which leadership is understood, and if we capture through research and theory that leadership is about 'shared or invented meanings within an organization' then we can reveal the work of teachers in other ways than as functions within a chain of command (Harris 2003, p. 314). This is an important perspective because the idea of teachers as leaders in their classrooms is officially endorsed by the DfES, but it remains the case that it is being defined in terms of the hierarchy:

> To achieve their full potential, teachers need to work in a school that is creative, enabling and flexible. And the biggest influence is the Head. Every teacher is a leader in the classroom. Every Head must be the leader of these leaders. And the Head's greatest task is the motivation and deployment of their key resource: staff. (DfES 2003b, p. 26)

The modernization of teachers through the remodelling of the school workforce is acknowledging the functional and organizational position of the teacher as leader of a classroom, who is to be externally motivated by a hierarchical superior and is used as a resource to deliver organizational outcomes. This is consistent with the first reading of the title of this book: teachers must be led and so we must focus on the models of leadership that enable them to be effectively and efficiently led. As the modernization policy continues to roll out, we need to ask questions about the knowledge claims underpinning this conceptualization of the teacher and seek to explore the possibilities for Leading Teachers as leaders of learning.

Knowledge and knowing

Mapping what we know about Leading Teachers requires a conceptual framework, and in providing this I intend to draw on and extend work done with Peter Ribbins (Gunter and Ribbins 2002a, 2003a,b; Ribbins and Gunter 2002; Ribbins and Zhang 2003). Our development of this framework is evolving, and I do not intend to settle the debate once and for all in this text. We are both indebted to the field for engaging with our work and providing important feedback to stimulate new insights (Gunter and Ribbins 2002b,c). Our approach in supporting mapping the field is based on the following intentions:

> First, to be topographical, so that the relief or underlying knowledge claims of the field can be described and theorized. Second to be geographical, so that positions and positioning on the surface and into the bedrock of knowledge claims can be charted and understood. Third, to be political, so that boundary drawing, entry and border skirmishes can be recognized

> and explained. Fourth, to be practical, through which the purposes of exploration can be enabled by charting route ways and erecting signposts. (Gunter and Ribbins 2002a, p. 387)

Conceptualization is concerned with knowledge, knowing and knowers, and so it is about what we know and need to know, what is worth knowing, how we know and practice that knowing, and who does the knowing. The dynamics of this are multilevel: (1) *technical*, through which we ask questions about teachers and their work; (2) *illuminative*, through which we ask questions about meaning such as the role of teachers in a school; (3) *critical*, through which we ask questions about power relationships within and external to the organization; (4) *practical*, through which we ask questions about improvement; and (5) *positional*, through which we align our research with particular knowledge claims and the epistemic communities that sustain them. For myself I intend to conceptualize Leading Teachers using this multilevel perspective, and through it I will be revealing how others approach the conceptualization of teachers as leaders. With this in mind I present Figure 2.1 as a knowledge framework through which Leading Teachers is located.

	Activity		
Challenge	***Understanding meanings*** *Conceptual*: challenging and developing understandings of ontology and epistemology. *Descriptive*: challenging and developing understandings of activity and actions	***Understanding experiences*** *Humanistic*: gathering and using experiences to improve practice. *Aesthetic*: appreciating and using the arts to enhance practice.	**Provision**
	Working for change *Critical*: revealing injustice and emancipating those who experience injustice. *Axiological*: clarifying the values and value conflicts to support what is right.	***Delivering change*** *Evaluative*: measuring the impact of role incumbents on outcomes. *Instrumental*: providing strategies and tactics for effectiveness.	
	Actions		

Figure 2.1 Knowledge and knowing in education

The framework is an example of what Gunter and Ribbins (2003b, p. 260) regard as a 'loose' typology designed 'to aid thought rather than replace it', because it is a 'good working beginning for anyone trying to understand what characterises and distinguishes the modes of enquiry in the field and what watersheds of assumption and world-views divide them' (Greenfield and Ribbins 1993, p. 179). While each quadrant has distinctive features that make it useful to how we understand our work about knowledge production, as the unfolding analysis will show, there are underlying complexities that need to be respected.

Figure 2.1 is structured with a vertical axis representing how we position ourselves in relation to thinking in abstraction and in ways that are distant, and thinking in action in ways that are proximate to the here and

Activity			
Challenge	***Understanding meanings*** *Conceptual:* • What does it mean to be and to do leaders, leading and leadership? *Descriptive:* • What do we see when we witness leaders, leading and leadership?	***Understanding experiences*** *Humanistic:* • What experiences do those involved in educational institutions have of leaders, leading and leadership? *Aesthetic:* • What can the arts do to illuminate the practice of leaders, leading and leadership?	**Provision**
	Working for change *Critical:* • What happens when power is exercised as leaders, leading and leadership? *Axiological:* • What does it mean for leaders, leading and leadership to support what is right and good?	***Delivering change*** *Evaluative:* • What impact do leaders, leading and leadership have on organizational outcomes? *Instrumental:* • What type of leaders, leading and leadership are needed to secure organisational effectiveness?	
Actions			

Figure 2.2 Knowledge and knowing in the field of educational leadership

now. The horizontal axis represents the purposes of activity and action, and how we seek to problematize through challenge and provide through delivery. We engage with this framework in the present to construct what is, and this is supported by our knowledge of the past and our speculations of and strategies for what might be.

Figure 2.2 develops our thinking through a prime focus on the field of educational leadership. It asks us to examine (1) who and what are leaders in relation to organizational, professional, social and personal identities? (2) what does it mean to do leading and what do we experience and witness what is and what might be done? and (3) how do we characterize leadership in regard to both formal leaders and leading, and to leadership within social practice?

Read together, Figures 2.1 and 2.2 have the potential to enable us to ask some serious questions about knowledge, knowers and knowing regarding Leading Teachers. Understanding meanings is *philosophical*, where conceptual and descriptive approaches are located in the concern to understand knowledge and knowing. This problematizes knowledge claims and is cognitive and affective as an activity distant from taking the actions that the knowledge claims may propose. We could ask: what does Leading Teachers mean? What does Leading Teachers look like? Understanding experiences is similarly about distance but with a view to improving practice, hence the focus is on accounts of practice by practitioners and how the arts can illuminate this and enable us to be *artful*. We could ask: what experiences have teachers had of Leading Teachers? What representations do we have (e.g. stories, artefacts) that can illuminate knowing about Leading Teachers? Working for change and delivering change are both closer to action, are ideological and require political commitment. The former is where critical and axiological approaches are located, and as such they seek to problematize with a view to *working for* change. We could ask: how might power structures act as a barrier to Leading Teachers? How do we work for Leading Teachers as a right and a good in our society? Delivering change is where evaluative and instrumental approaches are located, and the emphasis is on *securing outcomes*. We could ask: what do we know about the impact of Leading Teachers on organizational outcomes? What do teachers need to do in order to be and do Leading Teachers?

When we are concerned with understanding meanings we think, we engage in dialogue, we seek clarification, we problem pose more than problem solve. Playing with and developing ideas is an activity, but it does not necessarily determine or influence here-and-now actions. Similarly, when we work for change we do all of this, and we make a conscious political commitment through our actions to put the meanings into action. When we seek to understand experiences we want to listen to others' experiences and we can use the arts to provide ways of improving practice. When we need to deliver change we make a conscious political commitment to undertake the strategies for effective action. We problem solve more than problem pose.

Figures 2.1 and 2.2 represent praxis as 'morally committed action' (Carr 1993, p. 168) through which the binaries that are used to divide can be eliminated. First, our agency to do what we do and think what we think is not artificially separated from the social, political and economic structures (both systemic and organizational) that impact upon and are shaped by that agency. Those who focus on action (working for change and delivering change) may amplify structures that they want to reinforce or overcome, but their exercise of agency is implicated within those structures. Those who focus on activity (understanding meanings and understanding experiences) may promote their own and others' agency, but their understandings are structured by the systems and organizations they inhabit over time. Second, theory and theorizing are integral to practice, and vice versa. Taking action to work for change and to deliver change is based on theory and is itself theoretical. Similarly, as we are concerned with understanding meanings or seek to understand experiences, we may theorize as an activity that lacks immediate proximity to the doing, but the very nature of thinking, talking and breathing is itself made up of actions. Connected with this is the third point in which we do not separate out or privilege either intellectual or operational work. The activity of challenging is more intellectual than operational, but it still requires the doing and the evidencing of the doing through writing and talking. Conversely, the action of delivering change could be more operational than intellectual but it does require cognitive and affective processes as well as the public expressions through writing plans and chairing meetings. Fourth, all academics are practitioners because they do practice that is about the goals of an organization, and all practitioners are academics because they think about and are committed to goals that exceed and extend those of the organization.

In the four sections that follow, the knowledge and knowing underpinning the conceptual framework illustrated in Figures 2.1 and 2.2 will be further explained.

Understanding meanings

Knowledge and knowing about Leading Teachers through conceptual and descriptive approaches manifests itself through the teacher doing *philosophical* work about what they do and how they understand themselves and others through doing it. Teaching is essentially philosophical and is concerned with the what, why, when and how of knowledge, knowing and knowers. Teaching, when integrated into schooling, is a planned and intentional activity that is relational, mutual, purposeful and core to life. Consequently, teaching is more than a means and instead it needs to be understood as '*a distinctive way of being human* in a world that is now one with an unprecedented plurality of life-styles, value orientations and careers' (Hogan 2003, p. 209, author's own emphasis). We can develop this further by building on Noddings (2003) and arguing that teaching must (1) 'be constructed around the perceived need for learning' (p. 242), and this dependency on learning means that teaching 'does not exist for itself' (p. 242); (2) 'we can hardly insist that every student must learn what the teacher "teaches"' (p. 243), and so there is a productive tension between the intention of planned interventions in the lives of students with being able to respond to open-ended and unpredictable outcomes of interventions; (3) 'it is not the subjects themselves that induce critical thinking, but the ways in which they are taught and learned' (p. 246), with teachers making choices on methods and resources based on a respect for students as knowers combined with a need to care:

> It matters to students whether or not they like and are liked by their teachers. The teacher as person is centrally important in teaching. A physician can concentrate entirely on treating her patients; so long as she exercises the virtues that reflect her expertise, her personal character and personality matter very little. But the teacher sets an example with her whole self – her intellect, her responsiveness, her humour, her curiosity … her care. (Noddings 2003, p. 244)

Teaching exceeds subject knowledge and expertise:

> Working with young children, good teachers are keenly aware that they might have devastating effects or uplifting effects on their students. Some of these effects last, or at least are remembered, for a lifetime. This first great good of teaching – response-ability and its positive effects – is clearly relational. Teaching is thoroughly relational, and many of its goods are relational: the feeling of safety in a thoughtful teacher's classroom, a growing intellectual enthusiasm in both teacher and student, the challenge and satisfaction shared by both in engaging new material, the awakening

sense (for both) that teaching and life are never-ending moral quests (Noddings 2003, p. 249).

Hence learning is not just purchasing knowledge and skills, but is about how learning in context can exceed that context and so pupils may 'acquire intellectual and moral virtues that are goods in their own lives and in those of their friends and communities' (Dunne 2003, p. 368). If we are to proceed on this basis then what it means to be human is a central question for teachers, and as Starratt (2003) argues, we need as teachers to develop a sense of purpose based on (1) 'autonomy' not as isolation but as 'taking responsibility for what one does'; (2) the fact that being 'connected' is about 'social living' underpinned by a moral code, expectations, heritage and the environment; and, (3) 'transcendence ... is what leads us to turn our life toward someone or toward something greater than or beyond ourselves' (pp. 137–8).

Such an approach helps teachers not only to examine the meaning of their work and identity but also to be able to have a model of self and activity that is defendable when faced with externally determined demands for change. It is not being advocated that teachers should necessarily resist and be oppositional, but because of their relational and moral role with learners they have a responsibility to be in control of their practice and to engage in dialogue about other forms of that practice. They need to be powerful through knowing what they are doing and why they are doing it, and what the intended and possible unintended outcomes are. This is of interest when we come to read the texts about teacher leadership, and as Leithwood (2003, p. 114) asks, what is the 'motivation for grafting the concept of "leadership" onto the concept of "teacher"'? We might ask what does leadership do for teachers and what do teachers as leaders do for leadership? Is it about relabelling of activity for status purposes, or does it relate to the nature of activity? (Gunter 2004). Katzenmeyer and Moller (2001, p. 4) tell us that 'teachers are hesitant to be called leaders even when they are active in leadership activities', and they go on to argue that this could be due to (1) a perceived skills and knowledge deficit; (2) they don't want to be elevated above their colleagues; (3) they are not allowed to lead because of the audit and testing culture. However, it could be that teachers are exercising their agency in resisting a structuring label that represents knowledge claims about leadership as an organizational and hierarchical function. Doing philosophical work enables teachers to recognize that leadership is a relational activity within teaching, and so why not call it teaching? In this sense we are talking about Leading Teachers as both individual and social in how they conceptualize and practise their work, and so in meeting claims regarding their work as teacher leadership they will describe and analyse in order to clarify and justify, but they will also seek to argue from and for a particular position. This may be done in private on their own or with others, or in a more open setting of a professional development session.

Responses by teachers will most certainly be shaped by the way in which teacher agency to engage with philosophical questions has been negatively regarded by successive governments in England, and so it is possible that teachers may publicly reject and privately retain philosophical work as a means of handling this. Smyth (2001) illuminates this position when he describes how teachers have been criticized for professional autonomy or 'privatism' and, as a consequence, can be reluctant to engage in collegial or collaborative activity:

> When teachers retreat behind the closed door and play 'catch me if you can' games with administrators, then they are enacting a time-honored and very effective form of resistance, knowing full well that the costly surveillance apparatus necessary to control them is impossible to create. At the same time, they are also accommodating to a system that would fragment them and treat them as individuals competing against one another, rather than risk the danger of public displays of solidarity. Second, the danger in allowing the argument of teacher privatism to stand ... is that it is not only excessively harsh on teachers, but it is too deterministic in its denial of the importance of teacher agency and the possibility of teachers developing a collaborative culture to pursue progressive educational ends. None of this is to deny, of course, that some school administrators can (and do) use teacher isolation as a very effective means of divide and rule to protect their own power. (p. 105)

There is much to be gained by preventing philosophical work by teachers and so positioning them as seditious. Teachers will not accept their work as organizational leadership if they understand their own and other's work in a particular way, and they cannot become leaders if the organizational cultures and structures deny them this interpretation. Similarly, teachers will not automatically share work if the way a school is organized denies authentic collegial practice. We need to think deeply about these matters, not as an indulgence but in order to enable us to respect our need for meaning:

> Philosophy matters profoundly ... without it we are more likely to be ignorant or confused about what we are doing or intending and why; we are more likely to pursue problems that do not deserve our attention and/or attend too little to those that do; and we are likely to deny the possibility of

wisdom and justice in favour of a purely technical and therefore pointless proficiency. In other words, without philosophy education policy is more likely to be muddled and inconsistent, overly concerned with the tangential or the trivial, and so tremendously busy with getting things done that the possibility of foolishness outweighs the likelihood of wisdom. (Fielding 2000, p. 377)

Understanding experiences

Knowledge and knowing about Leading Teachers through humanistic and aesthetic approaches manifests itself through the teacher as a *lived, living* and *working life*. This approach enables us to recall our experiences and reflect on the meaning of our work through the construction of narratives. Such narratives are biographical through which we recall and seek to understand by storytelling, and these stories give access to the traces of human experience of events and processes, and enable understanding of identities, meanings and dispositions. This is not only an intellectual engagement with lived experience but also the emotional aspect of living in a complex world. Polkinghorne (1995) describes the importance of stories in which the narrative recognizes the challenges of exercising agency through events, sequences, discontinuities, chance and motivations within a context. In this sense action is 'emplotted' (Erben 1993) through which people create and live within a narrative structure that gives sense to their lives. Life events do have coherence in which stories have a beginning, an end, sequencing and selection. Human experience can be routine, habitual, but also problematic, and Denzin (1989) calls the latter *epiphanies* 'or moments of revelation in a person's life' (p. 71). The significance of stories means that the interaction between the person and work remains integrated, and is a space where dialogue about the self can productively take place.

Our engagement with the self is further enriched by aesthetics through which drama, painting, literature, photography, sculpture and music illuminate who we are, feel we are and might become. Hence artfulness is 'being learned or wise; or having practical skills (one who is dextrous and clever); or being skilful (adroit or cunning) in adapting means to ends or actions to purposes' (Ribbins and Zhang 2003, p. 4). Furthermore, exposure to the arts and 'unsafe authors' (Rapp 2002) can help to reveal the context in which we find ourselves:

> We must insist that passionate, creative, intuitively divergent, and heretical thinkers are heard in educational leadership programmes ... By engaging the living arts and unauthorized prophets, opportunities, discussions,

theories, and actions arise that lead to the dismantling of the undemocratic frameworks that manipulate our professional and personal lives. (pp. 183–4)

It is not argued that the arts provide decoration for a theory or a data set but challenge in ways that are in Greenfield's words 'humane' because 'the arts speak to questions of how to live a life' (Greenfield and Ribbins 1993, p. 257).

We can approach our working lives as 'history in person' by focusing on: 'relations between subjects' intimate self-making and their participation in contentious local practice' (Holland and Lave 2001, p. 5). This enables us to acknowledge that stories are a political process because 'a story is never just a story' but 'is a statement of belief and of morality' (Goodson 1995, p. 56) and so there are conscious and unconscious silences and noises related to how we engage with our agency to story and to understand the implications of our stories. There is an increasing amount of material that presents teachers' stories of their work and here I intend to present three examples to illustrate the dimensions of the process.

Sikes (1997; 2001) has collected stories of parents who teach:

When I had Becci it all changed. I'd always loved my children, the kids in the class I mean, but when I went back after the maternity leave, I was fierce. Like a mother tiger! There's that thing about mother-teachers having only half an eye on the job because their primary commitment is to their family. Well, of course it is, but that doesn't mean you slack up at school. With me it was the opposite because now I wanted the best for all the kids because I wanted Becci's teachers to give her the best when she went to school. It was almost a superstitious thing really, a sort of silly insurance policy. I work so much harder on planning and preparation and actual teaching in the classroom. I'm totally bushed when I get home at night. I'd say that my 'performance' has got better and better – and it's not just because I'm more experienced, its because of Becci. I'm not saying it will last, mind you, but that's how it is now. (Sikes 2001, p. 92)

Lingard *et al.* (2003) examine how racism is confronted:

You see it so often with lots of children that they're actually ashamed of being Aboriginal because they don't know enough about it to realize that it's something to be extremely proud of, you know. Like, a lot of white people think, well, what's acceptable is something that you see on a tea towel with a bloody spear and one leg up, or drinking and fighting in the streets. And you can't blame the kid for not wanting to identify with that. So through those types of lessons in Aboriginal studies, I try to get kids to say, 'Yes, we're black, we're Aboriginal, we're proud. If you have a problem with that, that's your problem, not mine. And I mightn't go drinking in the street or whatever, I mightn't be living in the bush or whatever, but I'm Aboriginal and I know who I am and I'm really proud of that.'

The other thing is, I think for too long we – all of us Aboriginal people – have, instead of facing up for a fight, it's always just been easier to lie down and get walked on. And I used to do that when I was at school, you know. I refuse to do it any more now, and I refuse to take the easy way out and not bother. And sometimes you do, because for your own sanity, not bother to take up an argument about racism or stuff like that, and sometimes it's not even worth it. For these kids here, I'd like them powerful enough in their minds to be able to not let people shit on them and get away with it, you know. (pp. 92–3)

Gronn (2003a) presents data from an interview with a Leading Teacher:

9. GRONN: Do you enjoy doing the role?

10. LT#4: Sometimes it's a lot of hard work, but there is a certain amount of satisfaction getting, at the start of the year when everything works, or you hope that everything works. You don't get too many thanks from the staff members, they, they sort of come and complain when things aren't going their way but, you, they expect it all to work properly and they've got their classes in the rooms they want, and so you usually only hear the complaints rather than anything positive, but, but I … I would now take the fact that if, the less people come and complain the better it is.

11. GRONN: So, to have it all in place when the gong goes at the start of day one … to have it all in place and ready to go, ready to rock and roll, how much work, I mean what, what does it entail for you to do that, I mean you are obviously working on it now, I suppose?

12. LT#4: Yeah, well at the moment I'm working on it full time for the next, the next two weeks, and I've been fairly flat chat [i.e. very busy] since about October.

13. GRONN: Is that right?

14. LT#4: Yeah, I've been planning. You know, before that, like the term break we had five staff turn over, so that was sort of, change in itself, but basically this term is fairly heavy going, but I still won't be able to get it finished before the end of the year because we won't have our staffing finalised. Like today, I found out that another staff member is leaving, so we won't have all our staff till January, so I will be here for the last couple of weeks of the holidays.

15. GRONN: So, I mean you, you won't have firm, when do you get firm Year 7 enrolment numbers?

16. LT#4: They are very accurate quite early. The junior school coordinator and the Year 7 teachers go out and they do a, visit the local primary schools and they, all the grade 6 kids, have to put their applications in and they are all processed by sort of, early October I suppose.

17. GRONN: Right, yeah, well that's okay then.

18. LT#4: So you, those numbers might increase by.

19. GRONN: Your numbers are fairly, so it's really the staffing variable that's the unknown, isn't it?

20. LT#4: Yeah, and we can model how much, what the retention rate is from year to year, so we roughly know that if we've got 300, say 300 Year 10s, we know that we'll have about 78 per cent of those next year. So we, going on previous retention rates we can plan for those (Gronn 2003a, pp. 271–2).

What can these types of accounts do for us? All the teachers represented through these extracts are talking about the self, and how through their agency they are showing a commitment to people and to the work that supports those people. We can witness what it means to be a teacher and to do teacherly things, and the dialogic interplay between professional and personal identities. Sikes (2001) argues that the mother who teaches is talking about performance management and questions the epistemology underlying predictions based on direct cause-and-effect connections and the measurement of impact. How we feel about our work, and how that is related to our wider and deeper selves, is embodied, and this shapes how we conceptualize and practise what we do. Gronn (2003a) shows how data presents the realities of work in its day-to-day setting, or 'the unromantic nature of the unrelenting hard grind endeavour associated with LT#4's role' (p. 272). Such work is being defined (in policies and in leadership textbooks) as management as distinct from leadership because LT#4 does the nitty gritty of making things work rather than have a strategic vision and mission. Gronn (2003a) asks 'how meaningful is such a resource/emotion divide' (p. 273) because the account shows the integration of vision with action, and by labelling such work in a particular way it enables some work to count more than others. What is being developed through these stories are matters to do with values and valuing. Lingard *et al.* (2003) illustrate how we can value the self through how our agency to act interplays with social structures, such as racism, that we experience and take action on. In this way the effective teacher is not the technician who implements a curriculum but a political and politicizing actor who is deeply embedded in the development of the student self.

A concern about this type of work is the potential separation of the lived life from the context in which it has been and is being lived. We might have many hundreds of stories that are worthy, but we might ask: what are they worth in relation to our knowledge of teaching? We might also be complicit in the structures that are shaping the lives in the story if we do not give recognition to those structures (Goodson 1995). Being reflective is not a guarantee of liberty, but could be a benign but nevertheless disciplinary process. Sikes (1997) describes how we might usefully and morally position ourselves on this:

> A major criticism centres around the significance that has been accorded to personal experience in much feminist research. Obviously, accounts of women's personal experience are essential if dominant interpretations are to be challenged but ... these must be contextualised otherwise the picture that is presented can be determinist and essentialist. It is also the case that personal stories can seem trivial and fictional ... For me at least, the purpose of using stories is not to offer 'objective truths', but rather to present very specific and contextual interpretation. This interpretation takes account, not only of the content of stories, but also of the influences which have led to them being told in particular ways. (pp. 19–20)

Stories are not just accounts of events, but reveal our dispositions regarding how we work our way through tough situations. Hence, the interplay between a policy as an official story about teachers and the storied accounts within policy by teachers is where Leading Teachers is located. Leading Teachers do leading through how they as individuals and with others articulate their lives and work.

Delivering change

Knowledge and knowing about Leading Teachers through evaluative and instrumental approaches manifests itself through the writing and promotion of *teacher leadership*. This is characterized as organizational, and is firmly located within the school effectiveness and improvement positions within the field.

Teacher leadership is organizational and is defined as the activity and actions that leaders in their role take in order to meet organizational goals. Teachers as leaders are positioned by hierarchy, and as organizational leaders they replicate that hierarchy. This is often regarded as a positive development because it enables site-based management reforms to work and to work better (Clemson-Ingram and Fessler 1997; Marks and Louis 1999; Ovando 1996). If headteachers are transformational leaders who must have a vision and a mission in order to inspire and build commitment to the organization and to change, then teachers as leaders must be integrated into these control structures and cultures (Geijsel *et al.* 2003). This is increasingly known in England as school leadership, and control is secured through organizational structures (roles and job descriptions), cultures (compliance and commitment), and performance (integrating cognitive and emotional processes), and so teacher leaders deliver. Descriptions of this are benign and optimistic:

> ... teacher leaders are strongly committed to their schools, the profession and the welfare of students. They have a positive orientation to their work, a sense of humour, and are warm, dependable and self-effacing. Teacher leaders are open and honest with their colleagues and students, and have well-honed interpersonal and communication skills. In addition, they possess the technical and organizational skills required for programme improvement and use them in concert with a broad knowledge based about education policy, subject matter, the local community and the school's students. Armed with a realistic sense of what is possible, these people actively participate in the administrative and leadership work of the school. They are viewed as supportive of others' work and model those practices valued by the school. (Leithwood *et al.* 2003, p. 195)

Organizational teacher leadership is defined first as formal, in which teachers are titled and have a job description: 'Lead teacher, master teacher, department head, union representative, member of the school's governance council, mentor – these are among the many designations associated with formal teacher leadership roles' (Leithwood 2003, p. 104); and, second as informal, in which teacher leaders work as members of the organization: 'by sharing their expertise, by volunteering for new projects and by bringing new ideas to the school' (Leithwood 2003, pp. 104–5). Empirical work is about using clear definitions to design studies that measure the impact of teacher leadership:

> Evidence from a large-scale survey indicated that both principals and teachers had a significant influence on most aspects of the school organization but some aspects were typically influenced more by those in one role rather than another. The independent influence of teacher leaders was strongest (and stronger than the principals' influence) with respect to school improvement planning, and school structure and organization. Principal leadership exercised its strongest independent influence on school improvement planning and school structure and organization, as well as on school mission and school culture. Furthermore, teachers were more likely to associate their principals than their teacher-leader colleagues with effective management and transformational leadership. (Leithwood *et al.* 2003, p. 195)

The aim is to move from support for this change and small-scale qualitative case-studies to large-scale testing (Leithwood 2003; Leithwood and Jantzi 2000). Such work takes time, and it is argued that reform cannot wait for large-scale 'effects' studies to take place, and so belief in teacher leadership as a good thing remains a strong driver for change. In particular, it is argued that teachers may not be aware of the potential in their work and the evidence base for school improvement (Leithwood and Jantzi 1999). Advocates resolve this by focusing on what principals can do to enable teacher leadership to develop, and Leithwood (2003) identifies that the development of teacher leadership is consistent with transformational leadership. Hence, while those who take this position could be seen to have things in common with *working for change* with a focus on progress, the difference is that the underlying conceptualization of improvement is organizational rather than social.

Teacher leadership in the English context is very much influenced by the work done in the USA and Canada, particularly the focus on knowing about the conditions through which schools can improve. In reviewing the literature on teacher leadership, Harris and Muijs (2002) identify six activities of teacher leadership that seem to integrate the formal and informal:

- continuing to teach and to improve individual teaching proficiency and skill;
- organizing and leading peer review of teaching practices;
- providing curriculum development knowledge;
- participating in school-level decision-making;
- leading in service training and staff-development activities;
- engaging other teachers in collaborative action planning, reflection and research. (p. 21)

Frost and Durrant (2003) are

> interested in the exercise of leadership beyond the boundaries arising from hierarchical models of organisation and traditional views of teachers' roles; it is not just a matter of delegation, direction or distribution of responsibility, but rather a matter of teachers' agency and choice in initiating and sustaining change whatever their status. (p. 174)

They go on to argue that teachers cannot do this themselves, but must be enabled. Externally, university departments of education can support teacher research, critical discourse and networking. Internally, transformational leadership is essential to enabling teachers to do things because heads have a grip on the levers of power [and] our recent research suggests that the impact of teacher-led development work can be radically transformed when senior colleagues work with teachers to ensure that the initial planning of such work addresses a wide range of possible outcomes including the development of teachers' personal capacity, the school's organisational capacity and pupils' learning. (p. 182)

The organizational conditions for this form of teacher leadership remains hierarchical, and recently it is this aspect that the field in England is beginning to grapple with. Harris (2004) gives recognition to the importance of what teachers do as teachers, which is distinct from what post-holders do, and as such the ability to separate out and control hierarchical roles as variables to be measured comes into question.

Working for change

Knowledge and knowing about Leading Teachers through critical and axiological approaches manifests itself through the teacher as *policy-maker*. Leading Teachers as policy-makers (rather than as policy-takers) enables the interplay between activity and action to be firmly located in the experiences and aspirations of teachers. Working for change draws on philosophical questions that are axiological by focusing on: what is good, and what is right? Such questions are vital to decision making, and as Hodgkinson (1996) states: 'unreflective action is degenerative. It is entropic.' He goes on to argue:

Policymaking cannot occur *tabula rasa*. Each policymaker arrives at the table already prejudiced and predisposed. Any myth of impartiality is akin to the illusion of scientific objectivity. Any decision entails values and any single decision maker embodies an a priori value complex. When policy is being formed or, in other words, when organizational philosophy is being established, what happens is that a factual scenario is *re*-presented to the policy makers with more or less logical consistency and empirical accuracy. Included in this representation, explicitly or tacitly, is a projection of hypothetical future state of affairs. This is then subjugated to the value considerations of the policy making administrators. That is, to their desires, wills, and intentions. Thus, through complex and subtle processes, as well as simple and direct mechanisms, agendas conflict and interact, and via dialogue, dialectic, and power the purposes, aims, objectives, and goals of the organization come to be formulated. An actual organizational value complex evolves which, regardless of the formulation or verbalization or rhetoric in which it is couched, becomes the mundane, quotidian philosophy that is translated into the realities and events of the workaday world through managerial processes. (p. 11)

The power dimensions in this policy process means that those who work for change argue that policy-making is a place where values should underpin purposes. Ozga (2000a) makes her position on this clear: '... my understanding of policy is that it is struggled over, not delivered, in tablets of stone, to a grateful or quiescent population' (p. 1). The link between challenge and action is interplayed through conceptualizing the teacher and pedagogic work as active and educational research as socially critical because 'education policy research should be available as a resource and as an arena of activity for teachers in all sectors because of its capacity to inform their own policy directions and to encourage autonomous, critical judgement of government policy' (p. 5).

There is some shared territory with the teacher-leadership work, and few would dispute the Katzenmeyer and Moller (2001) definition: 'teachers who are leaders lead within and beyond the classroom, identify with and contribute to a community of teacher learners and leaders, and influence others toward improved educational practice' (p. 5). What would be challenged is the labelling of this work in ways that insert a potential power-over structure (i.e. leader) that is disruptive and undermining of the development of pedagogic relationships within and external to the organization. For example, Cochran-Smith and Paris (1995) argue that mentoring may be constructed as teacher leadership, but without critical reflection on the power processes involved it remains 'a conservative activity that maintains the existing institutional, social and cultural arrangements of schools and schooling and eases the beginner into the prevailing norms of the local and larger professional culture' (p. 192). Furthermore, teachers working as leaders will bring them into new ways of working with headteachers that are complex and require us to understand micropolitical dimensions (Smylie and Brownlee-Conyers 1992) and how this is worked through does require a critical approach. Indeed, the emphasis on role in teacher leadership could be the means by which performativity triumphs in 'the struggle over the teacher's soul' (Ball 2003a, p. 217).

Positioning around teachers as policy-makers is based on how teachers' work is organized, and the relationship between teachers as workers and the state (Ozga 1995; Smyth 2001). The argument is that the choices teachers make in their practice are, unfortunately, less to do with pedagogy and more about the context in which they find themselves: 'the thrust toward school reform appears to be predicated on a degradation of the work of teachers, with the craft of teaching being replaced by a panoply of technical rational procedures' (Smyth 2001, p. 9). The teacher-leadership literature, which focuses to varying degrees on formal and informal organizational roles, is consistent with this because through the optimism of the teacher as change agent reform can be smoothly delivered. It is argued that by differentiating teachers into hierarchies of experts undermines other ways in which teachers can 'remake, and if necessary re-order, the world in which they and their students live' (Smyth 2001, p. 53). Consequently, teachers have been simultaneously sedated and stimulated: they have been calmed through the provision of ringbinders and laptops that store and provide prefabricated lessons and are exhorted to be excited and exciting about the performance delivery of those lessons (Gunter 2001).

Leading Teachers as policy-makers is 'an ethical stance' (Crowther 1997, p. 15) based on the exercise of agency rather than accepting work as 'ventriloquists for transnational capital' (Smyth 2001, p. 156). Research has gathered examples of how teachers, in new hard times, are still able to do Leading Teacher work by shaping learning (Lingard *et al.* 2003), and how we need to explain experiences of leadership in more sophisticated ways than through essentializing identities of those who have broken through the glass ceiling (Reay and Ball 2000). In reviewing the literature and presenting an analysis of teachers' work, Smyth (2001, pp. 171–2) argues that 'teacher learning, which is becoming increasingly coupled with teacher leadership, is about teachers not being fearful of "confronting strangeness"', through which teachers refuse 'to accept customs, rituals, and the familiar world unquestioningly', and so, 'teacher leadership is, therefore, about teachers understanding the broader forces shaping their work and resisting domestication and not being dominated by outside authorities'. It is also about recognizing that while teachers work in an organization called a school, it is first and foremost an institution created to enable schooling as a community orientated and inclusive activity that is political, and requires educationalists to work for socially just change.

Dynamics in Leading Teachers

How we engage with the framework and analysis presented in Figures 2.1 and 2.2 is core to how Leading Teachers is understood and practised both through action and advocacy of particular action. While the four quadrants are distinct they do interconnect, and in scanning the map we can see how qualitative data that enables humanistic experiential accounts to be gathered and interpreted can also be used in the other three sections. For example, those who work for change use stories to support action against social injustice (Helsby 1999), while those who deliver change use stories to prescribe how change should happen (Crowther *et al.* 2002). How we position ourselves regarding Leading Teachers is related to the choices we make through the exercise of agency, and so we reveal our habitus or dispositions to do and to be in the world. This agency is shaped through the wider political and social structures in which we are located, and so the field of educational leadership is characterized as an arena of struggle where we seek to position ourselves and others seek to position us (Bourdieu 2000). We must be mindful that our engagement with the knowers, knowing and knowledge of Leading Teachers is structured by metafields of political and economic interests. The Political Right and Left can be both impatient and excited about these positions, and those who work directly within the field can feel both pressured or supported by this:

> Educational administration's dilemma is part of a 'crisis of modernity'. The present that the Right and Left lament is ravaged by ignorance, moral decay, AIDS, crushing poverty, rape of the environment, human oppression of all descriptions, and international terrorism practised, simultaneously, by sophisticated armies and individual fighters. The Right's focus on public education has been generated by an illiterate and innumerate youth culture whose literature of choice is cyberpunk and whose primary intellectual loyalty is to the 'web'. In this Right-wing view of things educational administrators are bumbling functionaries. According to the Left, public education is a witting or unwitting co-conspirator in various oppressions, exclusions, and subordinations that are required by post-industrial capitalism. In this Left-wing critique educational administrators are immoralists. (Kaminsky 2000, p. 203)

While this characterization is about the USA, the illumination it provides can also be helpful in understanding the situation in England. While the drama can distort, it is still the case that those who lead, manage and administer education have been, and continue to be, the subject of criticism – often unfair and vicious criticism. My position is that Leading Teachers as delivering change through teacher leadership is being over-amplified because it is consistent with school effectiveness and school improvement. We need to give more recognition to Leading Teachers doing philosophy, story-telling and policy-making. Hence how we connect activity with action is the core issue for those who are concerned with the purposes and workings of our schools, and through an analysis of two interpretations of transformational leadership I intend to argue that this is demanding but necessary intellectual work.

Transformation as the core purpose of leadership practice dominates the current preoccupation with what teachers should do and what

Activity			
Challenge	**Understanding meanings** Developing meanings of transformation at individual, group, organization and societal levels.	**Understanding experiences** Gathering experiences of individual, group, organization and societal transformation.	**Provision**
	Working for change Working for socially critical transformation through political relationships based on activism.	**Delivering change** Delivering organizational transformation in order to secure educational reforms.	
Actions			

Figure 2.3   The dynamics of transformational leadership

should be done with (or even to) teachers. The word 'transformation' is used in everyday terms to mean change in appearance and substance, or metamorphosis. When related to leaders, leading and leadership it can be represented as shown in Figure 2.3.

Understanding meanings enables teachers to ask what change means and what it could mean for themselves and others. Teachers can understand experiences by focusing on what we know about change for themselves and for others. I intend to focus on how the understanding of meanings and experiences are differently drawn upon to characterize the practices required to act in a transformational way if Leading Teachers are to work for change and/or deliver change. This is illustrated in Figure 2.4 and presents a summary of the main features of how transformational leadership is being differently conceptualized and how practice is understood.

Delivering change is based on a form of transformational leadership that has been developed in the private sector and is concerned with organizational control and production. The leader–follower binary divide is based on a covert and benign power-over process by the headteacher to the teacher:

Effective principals will model continuous learning while meeting the challenges of aligning organizational members' values and school vision and emphasising learning as a priority for teachers as much as for their students. System learning and improved performance depends on the increased efficacy of principals and teachers, as well as students … When

Characteristics	Working for change	Delivering change
Agency	Leadership is located in the development of the self and the relationships between agents with a focus on socially critical change. Vision is about interconnections with the past and possibilities for how we might want to live together in the future.	Leadership is located in the attributes and actions of role incumbents. The agency of the leader is used to control the agency of the workforce and clients through communicating and sustaining a vision and mission for organizational change.
Structure	Organizational and social structures interplay with agency in ways that shape, enhance and prevent. Agency is based on democratic values, and is orientated towards working for democratic opportunities and practices.	Agency of the workforce and clients is controlled through roles and processes based on authorized delegation and participation.
Meaning	Dialogue takes place about the history, purposes and power structures with the organization and how this interplays with meaning and action.	Agency of the workforce and clients is controlled through an organizational culture which promotes consensus and commitment. Meaning is given through the leader vision of the future.
Knowledge	Agency is developed through access to historical and social knowledge about the self and the community.	Agency of the workforce and clients is controlled through reflection and reflexivity on organizational practice individually and in teams.
Relationships	All can exercise leadership and the interplay between agents can enable formal responsibilities and secure support for individuals and groups.	Agency of the workforce and clients is controlled through contract compliance, individual interactions and emotional engagement.
Outcomes	Expectations are social and socializing, and are based on the dialectic of understanding antecedence and working for equity.	Agency of the workforce and clients is controlled through establishing a culture of expectations regarding organizational outcomes. Outcomes are performance measured and rewarded.

Figure 2.4   The change dimension in transformational leadership

teachers are empowered in areas important to them, they become a profession of learners who engage in inquiry, reflective practice and continuous problem-solving, and, at the same time build leadership capacity ... It is argued, therefore, that the level of formal and informal leadership roles assumed by teachers in any one school provides evidence of their capacity for learning, as well as leadership. (Silins and Mulford 2002, pp. 430–31)

I would argue that this is not transformational leadership because it does not work for social change. It does not confront issues of gender, sexual orientation, age, ethnicity and class as structural barriers regarding the capacity to learn and to exercise agency (Gunter 2001). While we must respect the need for organizations to function efficiently and effectively, we also need to question the power structures in which those organizations are located, and this can be done through leadership which, as Foster (1989, p. 57) argues, is 'a shared and communal concept':

> Leadership, then, is not a function of position but rather represents a conjunction of ideas where leadership is transferred between leaders and followers, each only a temporary designation. Indeed, history will identify an individual as the leader, but in reality the job is one in which various members of the community contribute. Leaders and followers become interchangeable (p. 49).

This conceptualization of transformational leadership is built on Leading Teachers as distributed practice that requires intellectual work. Learning and using that learning through association is more engaging than that proposed in delivering organizational change through teacher leadership. For example, Leithwood *et al.* (1999) present 'intellectual stimulation' as a feature of organizational effectiveness through reflection on work and performance:

> Leadership initiatives potentially having this effect might take many forms. Such initiatives can be quite informal and modest, for example, asking a teacher why he or she continues to use a routine that has become an unthinking, but not very useful, part of his or her repertoire. An example of a somewhat more extensive but still informal initiative aimed at intellectual stimulation would be attempting to persuade a teacher that he or she has the capacity and support to attempt new grouping practices or to take on new professional challenges, such as leading a school team, providing some professional development to colleagues or mentoring a novice teacher. A more formal and extensive example of intellectual stimulation would be engaging staff in the planning and implementation of a several-year professional development programme co-ordinated with the school improvement plan. (p. 75)

This intellectual activity is about production and is achieved through actions which structure controlled ideas and emotions. It is what Ball (2003a, p. 217) describes as teachers having to 'calculate about themselves, "add value" to themselves, improve their productivity, strive for excellence and live an existence of calculation'. It is also the type of leadership that Blackmore (1999) argues is a barrier to equity. An alternative way of being and doing in the world is working for change where we engage in intellectual work which is about respecting experiential knowledge, questioning existing practice, and having the courage to exercise judgement. Leading Teachers accept and resist the initiatives of others automatically to review their practice and declare it as deficient; as Smyth (2001) puts it:

> If teachers are to challenge and ultimately supplant ... [the] ... dominant technocratic view of schooling, then it is necessary that they be articulate about the nature of their work, and where they are located historically and pedagogically in it, while also being conscious of its social and political purposes. It means teachers going beyond the roles of technicians, managers, or efficient clerks imposed upon them by others, and being unwilling to continue to accept the way things are in schools. Even where these externally contrived agenda appear to be rational, sensible, and humane, the inability of management pedagogies to adequately understand, let alone grapple with, the complexities in classrooms creates a situation of opposition for teachers. What must not be overlooked is that unequal power relations in schools (between individuals and groups) are established and constructed through the lived experiences of people in schools. As such, they can be 'disestablished' and 'deconstructed' in the way people choose to live, work, and ultimately penetrate the object of their struggles. What is needed is faith in the power of teachers to reflect upon, resist, and change the oppressive circumstances in which they find themselves. (p. 203)

These matters require a wider and richer analysis of how power is ordered, sorted and used in educational organizations. This is particularly the case since distributed leadership is emerging as a powerful means of securing teacher leadership in ways that are pertinent to the arguments about Leading Teachers. I will discuss this further in the next chapter.

3   Leading Teachers as Distributed Leadership

The challenge for those who work in education is getting the work done, getting the right work done, and enabling a sense of purpose (for the self and the collective) to shape and sustain this work. And there is so much of this work to do. Recent governments have ensured that what counts as valid work is increasingly decided by non-teachers, and so evidencing the delivery of the work is regarded as vital to prove that the work is being done. Teaching and learning are located in such power structures and is itself a power structure, and yet much of this is elided from the ringbinders and lists of bullet-points of 'good' and 'effective' practice that is presented to teachers as *the* solution. The emphasis on getting teaching and learning right means that knowledge is packaged, transmitted and tested; the effective teacher is led by others who know better, and this is replicated in the classroom with the teacher who is licensed to know and the student who is in receipt of this knowing.

Another, but currently suppressed, tradition exists which emphasizes developing learning, and so teachers' work is activity concerned with designing, delivering and enabling structured and structuring learning experiences. This is focused on developing the student as self so that they know who they are, where they are, why they are there and how they might want to develop further. Teachers structure learning in ways that enable agency to develop; such structuring productively questions learning structures that the student brings to the process (e.g. family, community) and is itself challenged through the development of self. Through actions such as writing, talking, thinking, looking and listening, the teacher is able to work with and for the student as an individual and as a part of a collective. This is a complex process of knowing about what is established, what is conditional and what is emerging within and through learning. It is highly skilled work, but from the outside looking in it can look easy because it is often embodied and seemingly natural-ized. What makes work challenging, and for some impossible, is the contradictory situation that teachers find themselves in regarding how work is and should be organized. If teachers are to lead learning in ways that are meaningful then we need to examine the context in which their work is structured. In this chapter I intend examining how we understand power and its distribution.

Powerful work

The study and practice of education is about power. This is nothing new, but it is necessary to keep stating it because much of what we read about school leadership is concerned to replicate existing power structures in ways that sustain teachers as followers of organizational leaders. If we want to enable teachers in their work with learners to develop learning then we need to begin with how their agency is understood by the self and others, and how this agency is structured through structures such as the organization.

Power does not exist in the abstract but is lived by teachers in their practice, and has been defined 'as the ability to achieve a desired outcome' (Heywood 2000, p. 35). Hence teachers design desired outcomes through the teaching and learning process, and aim to achieve them through the interplay between their own agency and that of others. Teacher agency is about securing outcomes whilst recognizing that others' agency will shape this through acceptance, fudging and resistance. Hence power is formally located in the position of being a teacher with a job description and cultural expectations of what a teacher is or should be, and it is in the doing of teacherly activity and actions that power is exercised. As noted here this takes place within structures both in the school as an organization with its rules, conventions and culture, and in the wider context of the school as a publicly funded state institution and as a social organization within society. The politics of educational ambitions and interests are played out in schools as a site where the state is a key player regarding securing economic efficiencies and as the guardian of legality and morality. As an agency of the state the school is a place where competing interests are located and it is a focus of those interests. It is also a place where society is represented, where issues of class, race and sexuality emerge, and can be replicated.

Hence *where* decisions are made about education and about teachers' work is central to our analysis. If teachers make decisions about their work with and for students then we could focus on this relationship. But it is not that simple. Decisions about that relationship are made by those proximate to it such as the Leadership Team or the Governing Body, but also by those in local and national government, in national agencies such as Ofsted and the NCSL, and in international agencies such as the World Bank and the International Monetary Fund (IMF). The tensions we have to come to terms with focus around why teachers and students accept and dissent on these decisions, and how we understand the day-to-day relationships within these wider structuring forces. To do this we have to have a more sophisticated understanding of power than that assumed in much of what is written about in school leadership. We need to go beyond the dualism of the powerful and powerless. If we are to describe the workings of power and to present an argument by which Leading Teachers can happen differently to that being presented to them in official models, then we need to go to the intellectual roots of the field within the social sciences.

Power is both a 'power to' and a 'power over' relationship. It is power to achieve, directly or indirectly, wanted and unwanted outcomes (Dowding 1996; Heywood 2000). Heywood (2000) argues that there are 'different faces of power': (1) power as decision making or the 'conscious judgements that in some way shape actions or influence decisions' through 'intimidation', 'deal'-making and 'the creation of obligations, loyalty and commitment'; (2) power as non decision making or 'the ability to prevent issues or proposals from being aired'; and (3) power as 'thought control' or 'the ability to influence another by shaping what he or she thinks, wants or needs' (pp. 35–6). Dowding (1996) characterizes this power over others as 'social power' or 'the ability of an actor *deliberately* to change the incentive structure of another actor or actors to bring about or help to bring about outcomes' (p. 5, my emphasis). Such relations are 'dispositional' as we could exercise power in a particular way but may not, and so we should not assume a direct cause-and-effect relationship. A teacher could have the capacity to threaten a student with sanctions to enable work to be done, but may not do it and indeed may never do it during the whole of her career. A student may expect to be threatened and so has a range of responses to this, and if it does not happen is challenged to respond differently. Hence studying relationships in social contexts such as schools is difficult because there are underlying matters that may not be revealed such as how we attribute power and how this manifests itself privately and publicly through fear and joy.

Those trying to study the reality of and dispositions towards power can be those who are in or are potentially within the power relationship. Reading a situation and reacting or responding is key to how we proceed on a day-to-day basis. We have routines and habits that enable us to operate in ways where there is some degree of certainty, and we challenge those routines and habits when we want to make changes. Dowding (1996) argues that the word 'deliberate' is essential to understanding social power because your 'choice situation' is changed (p. 7) and so issues of cooperation and conflict emerge. Power to do something assumes that there is cooperation, whereas power over impacts on another's choice and means that conflict could be generated (Dowding 1996).

Power is therefore about influence, and this is tied up with a range of practices around authority, legitimacy, accountability and responsibility. Heywood (2000, p. 15) states that 'whereas power is the ability to influence the behaviour of others, authority is the right to do so', and so we obey because of a duty (moral and contractual) to accept that others have power over us. In a formal organization such as a school this is mainly evident in hierarchy, job descriptions and salary scales or *de jure* authority which 'operates according to a set of procedures or rules which designate who possesses authority and over what issues'. It can also be related to attributed authority where there are those who are *de facto* in authority because they have earned respect and/or expertise and so are 'recognised as being "an authority" by virtue of his or her specialist skills or knowledge' (pp. 15–16). Hence the exercise of power is legitimate because of claims to authority where what we privately believe is valid can be more important in understanding organizational life than through regular demonstrations of obedience.

Authority and legitimacy are tied to responsibility and accountability. If we have authority and claim legitimacy then we are also responsible first 'in the sense of being responsible *for* something or someone' and so as a teacher we work hard because we feel a personal and moral responsibility towards our students; and second, we are accountable or answerable 'in the sense of being responsible *to* someone' and so we must report to a 'higher authority' (Heywood 2000, pp. 145–6). In this way there is 'a duty to explain one's conduct and be open to criticism by another' not in an arbitrary way but through the necessary limitations in conduct created through appointment within an organization (i.e. job descriptions) and the rules created by particular groups (i.e. professional standards) (Heywood 2000, p. 117). So as teachers we answer to the headteacher (or his/her representative such as a head of department) for our work and we agree how the boundaries to that work are controlled. Within a professionally staffed organization such as a school there are peer relationships regarding working together, and it is possible that the headteacher is line-managed as a teacher by someone in the middle management, and so these boundaries are significant and complex. Self-control over work, in the sense of having autonomy to make decisions, is regarded as one of the fulfilling aspects of teaching, and it is seen as a necessity given the contextual nature of the power relationships involved between teacher and student as individuals, small groups and whole classes. Discretion and judgement are a product of training and education, and are controlled through responsibility *for* and *to* both formally by established performance procedures and informally through day-to-day interactions.

This discussion of power raises some vital issues for educational leadership. As Gronn (2003a) has argued:

> ... leadership is part of a family of terms of closely related usage, a number of which overlap in meaning, thereby suggesting possible redundancy. These terms are used to distinguish different modes of human conduct and engagement. Apart from leadership, the other members of this family or grouping are: authority, power, influence, persuasion, manipulation, coercion and force. Now, within this discursive family, leadership is the favourite and most prominent offspring, in both education and beyond. None of its siblings, it seems to me, have ever really commanded anything like the reverence and respect with which leadership has been adorned. To my way of thinking, however, this hallowed status is rather puzzling, for while leadership shares some of the defining attributes of its family members, it alone gets singled out for special treatment. (p. 274)

Indeed, Gronn (2003a) goes on to argue that if all the millions of words written about leadership actually do define it in this way then

> ... if it is influence we are really talking about, then why not stay with that word? Why do commentators feel the need to grace the influential conduct they have in mind with the status of leadership? In short, when describing and analysing the flow of collective action and the conduct of persons as part of that process, why is it leadership we are talking about rather than influence or power? (p. 277)

This is a very significant point. It supports the argument, already established in Chapter 1, that we need to be careful of books and training programmes that are about school leadership where the emphasis is on leadership in an educational organization. This model of leadership is about relabelling the exercise of power within schools in a benign and attractive way. It seems that we don't want to talk about power and influence because they are words that suggest manipulation, and if we told people directly that they were being trained to do manipulation and to be manipulated then it could be seen as distasteful. Using a label like leadership makes it attractive to those who do the influencing and those who are to be influenced because it enables activity and actions to be constructed in a positive way around organizational development. It is very hard to argue that you need not be led because to make this argument means that at best you will be characterized as eccentric and at worst a rebel who is undermining learning.

Educational leadership meets the issue of power head on and recognizes that how and why we conceptualize it is central to how we understand our work. The social sciences are there to be drawn on and developed through our work, not to be feared or ridiculed. The focus on power within teaching and learning can be understood as (1) within and about education rather than imported from a business setting (e.g. provider–client relationship); (2) the relationship is educational (i.e. the experience of working and living within the relationship enables learning to take place); and (3) it is underpinned by educational values regarding a mutual and reciprocal commitment to care and to social justice within learning and communities. Educational leadership is central to the process of teaching and learning, and we should be brave enough to call it teaching and learning. Leading Teachers are those who within teaching and learning exercise and are in receipt of the power *to* and *over*. Whether those who work within teaching and learning relationships (teachers, students, parents, wider communities) are currently able to do this given decades of being undermined will be developed further in Chapter 4. In the meantime, I intend now to move on to examining how teachers' work is organized through the historical legacy that is shaping the capacity to control and do Leading Teachers.

Organizing teachers' work

Teachers have to be highly self-motivated and organized people in order to prepare and enable learning in face-to-face contact for potentially 25 hours per week in the classroom, plus all the other contact through being a member of an educational community. How teachers' work is currently organized and the debates about how it might be better organized is structured through two trends identified by Grace (1995, p. 45): first as 'hierarchical and authoritarian' and second as 'shared decision-making'. The first trend is located in the headmasterly tradition of the nineteenth century and can be traced through to the entrepreneurial school leader from the 1990s onwards. The second is salient in the postwar drive for participation evident in professional cultures, and more recently by being reworked as teams and collaboration. These trends are juxtaposed within schools and located in social and political cultures where there is paradoxically enduring support for strong leadership but also a commitment to democratic ideals.

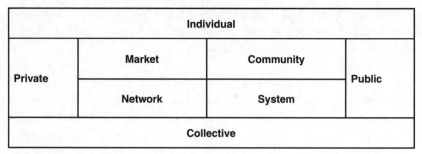

Figure 3.1 Organizing and organizations

We can understand the workings of these two trends through ways in which schools organize and can be organized, and the dimensions are outlined in Figure 3.1. The horizontal axis is concerned with whether, and to what extent, the purpose of organizing is for the public or the private; the vertical axis displays an orientation to the individual or the collective.

Teachers work in a *system* with a commitment to the public good oriented to the collective as participants and as beneficiaries of this structure. In the post-1945 era, agency was shaped by values that were universal and welfarist in provision for all, and the code that grew up to support this was that of a partnership between teachers as a profession and the community as democratic citizens through local governance. A school is not just an organization but primarily a public institution. Teachers are well-educated, trained and committed to teaching and their students, and are orientated to the emancipatory potential of teaching and learning as a means through which democracy can be further developed. Ways of working grew up that meant that the smooth running of the system depended on a disposition to care for and about, show goodwill, and the commitment of teachers to work until the job is done and not to leave a student or a colleague in difficulty. While democratic ideals could be worked for, this was always circumscribed by established structures and cultures regarding traditional norms about how schools should be run. The system has been differentially grafted on to a division of labour formally based on the dominance and unified structure of the headteacher with vertical and horizontal divisions of departments/faculties/houses, and enacted through roles and job descriptions. Hence we often experience the paradox of leaders, leading and leadership located in hierarchical traditions overlain and in tension with altruistic values and notions of peers and collegiality.

Teachers work in a *market* where we have inherited the nineteenth-century commitment to private interests located in the needs of the individual. Agency is shaped by values that are individual and individualizing in exclusive provision, and the code that grew up to support this is that of a contract between teachers as providers and consumers/investors as stakeholders within the school. Teachers are well-trained and committed to teaching and students, and are orientated towards delivering consumer-driven teaching and learning. Schools are small businesses that need to be efficiently, effectively and economically managed, and leadership of the school (usually known as transformational leadership) enables the headteacher to act as entrepreneur in the acquisition of resources. Within the school context the division of labour is based on a separation of the leadership team from those who deliver the education product, and the actual structures and processes are based on fitness for purpose through teams and task-groups. Teachers are empowered to deliver and be accountable for the vision and mission of the school through their performance on organizational targets and customer satisfaction. Hence leaders are those who are in formal roles with job descriptions, leading is what they do, and leadership is a contractual relationship between fellow workers where there is recognition that the individual can emerge as entrepreneur through teacher leadership.

Teachers work in a *community* where we have inherited the Anglo-Saxon commitment to the local good through an orientation to the individual as the means through which meaning is created and defended. Agency is shaped by values that are local and based on strong beliefs that unite the community, and the code that grew up to support this is that of an integration of boundaries around common interests and beliefs. Teachers are well-trained and committed to teaching and students, and are orientated towards teaching and learning that secure integration and balance. A vertical and horizontal structure is in place to secure accountability, but the emphasis is less on hierarchical direction and followership and more on self-following through agreed strategies. Hence moral purpose is about obligation and delivering what you promised, and so work is shared. The tensions between the commune and diversity, the collective and the private, are worked through by leadership as a mutual and reciprocal relationship. There is a community of learners and learning, and more specifically of practice, where meaning is developed and biographies are used in the delivery of change. The degree of tightness of control through belief means that community could be a loose association of likeminded people or a cult with tight boundaries that excludes more than it includes.

Teachers work in *networks* where we have inherited the medieval commitment to the enhancement of private interests through an orientation to the collective as participants and as beneficiaries of this structure. Agency is shaped by the pursuit of those interests, and the code that grew up to support this is that of negotiation and deal making within the setting of enabling a deal to be struck between diversity and the good of the whole. Teachers are well-educated, trained and committed to teaching and students, and are orientated not only to teaching and learning but to the promotion of their control over their work and interests. The formal organization of work may be structured through a hierarchy, a market, a community, but the informal structuring is based on micropolitics. Teachers will work to promote their interests in relation to the operation of both the external political demands within school and the internal political activity of how individuals and groups operate. Hence work can be delegated and shared, and people can be empowered, but within and between networks what work is done, how and by whom, is dispersed and concentrated depending on the deals that have been agreed either tacitly or formally. Hence, while a formal hierarchical structure is in place and all publicly swear fealty to the leader and his/her agents, it is also the case that there are leaders who may not have formal job descriptions as a role-incumbent; nevertheless, they do leading, and leadership is a political relationship between competing and cooperating interests. Such an understanding of work can be seen to be potentially negative through resistance and the formation of cultures that prevent cooperation, and Hoyle (1982, p. 87) describes this as the 'dark side of organizational life'. However, it is also recognized that through meaning-making and working for change dissent is a positive aspect where in peer communities (as distinct from line-management subordinate organizations) those who are colleagues and who know through their practice, are knowers within their practice and are knowledgeable from their practice, have the right and indeed responsibility to disagree. What makes organizational life simultaneously productively and unproductively challenging is the borderline between what is/is not bad behaviour and what is/is not professional conduct.

A teacher currently working in a school in any part of England, is experiencing contradictions arising from their work being structured as a system, a market, a community and a network. This is both in the descriptive sense of how we might observe a teacher in practice and in a normative sense in how we might experience a teacher being exhorted to change. It is the case that a system and a network are the two that have been focused on by those who wish to describe and critique practice. The system is regarded as bureaucratic and the network as provider capture, and both are regarded as self-serving. The two have often been conflated into the attack on teacher professionalism through which the state has guaranteed a job for life for people who are not working in the interests of parents, the taxpayer or the wider community. The market and the community are the two that have been focused on by those who wish to direct and change practice. The market is regarded as liberating in the sense that teachers can meet the needs of those they are meant to be working for and so have a job based on performance. The re-emergence of the market from the 1980s and into the 1990s is based on an attack on the system and network as a means of restructuring education as a private good to be commodified and sold. The overlaying of the market on to the postwar settlement of welfarism created a quasi-market in which new roles, work and cultures were brought into schools, but they did not eradicate the regulation by the state or the commitment to social justice. Unease with both the system and market approaches to education, and a desire to eliminate network politics, is leading to an emphasis on community through what is being labelled, in various ways, as distributed leadership. We need to examine the implications of this for our understanding of both descriptions and exhortations regarding how we work together, and how we articulate not only the location of power within organizations but also the exercise of power over each other.

Distributed leadership

Within this setting of contradiction and contest regarding the organization of work we are witnessing the promotion of leadership that is labelled as 'distributed', and as the previous section articulated, this form of distribution is currently being normatively characterized and promoted within the school as a community. Does distributed leadership help teachers to engage with their contradictory settings and provide a workable solution to structure their working lives? Will it enable teachers to embrace philosophical and experiential knowledge and knowing, and work for change? Will it enable teachers to develop a politics of practice so that wider social change can be worked for? These questions provide an interesting challenge for the field, and in this section I intend to examine how the field is approaching the theory and practice of distribution.

Jackson (2003) tells us about the vitality of distributed leadership:

> ... the current model for the school system in this country is not marked out by characteristics of learning, innovation, enquiry and knowledge

creation. The talk has been more of structures, job descriptions, targets and performance management. It will involve new ways of thinking about how schools function and not always within a climate that is conducive. Professional learning communities are distributed leadership communities. When community, cooperation and collaborative learning are the prevailing metaphors driving our schools, rather than hierarchy, competition and accountability, then it will follow that issues of voice, participation, ownership and active democracy will be precursors of new leadership patterns, and this is a hard road to travel. It is one of the journeys against the grain (p. xiii).

Indeed, it is further argued that to achieve distributed leadership requires understanding two paradoxes: first, a 'redesign' of schools needs distributed leadership to deliver this redesigning; and second, the development of distributed leadership is dependent on 'strong headteacher leadership' (p. xiv). However, a more fundamental issue is how distributed leadership is handled within the current educational context. Teachers are overworked, and may be doing work that others could do, but without changes to that work or to the workforce then they will have to continue to do it. Hence distributing work is not necessarily the answer. Furthermore, grafting distributed leadership onto educational organizations that are unitary and hierarchical means that those who are directly accountable, and hence face removal/resignation, may find it too risky to engage in distributed leadership. Wallace (2001) argues that in England headteachers need to proceed 'with caution towards the most extensive, equal sharing of leadership possible to maximise potential for synergy, while allowing for contingent reversal to hierarchical operation to minimise the risk of disaster' (p. 165). The key issue for the field is how it handles the optimism of the prescription of distributed leadership with the realities of the description of those who do the distributing and are distributed to.

Where does this leave us? Given that the work underpinning the learning of twenty or less children in the smallest schools to more than 1,500 in the largest schools is inevitably divided up, or shared, or distributed between people with different knowledge and skills, then we might ask: what is being distributed and how? There are a number of forms of distribution that are being presented, but all begin with the tiredness and inappropriateness of transformational leadership (and its hybrids) with the emphasis on the lone superhead who secures commitment through charisma and the powerful vision of the future. For those who have lived on this territory there is a growing realization that schools don't work like that after all, and that it is a model that is not very attractive to serving heads and is not inspiring others to become aspiring heads. For those who have always challenged this territory then there is the opportunity to have the debate about the realities of practice heard, and in particular that work goes on and will go on to a high standard without leader or leadership activity and actions.

There seem to be three interlinked 'distinctive elements' that are emerging as research and debate continues within the field. Bennett *et al.* (2003) identify them as follows:

- Leadership is not located in the individual but is 'an emergent property of a group or network of interacting individuals' and through this dynamism 'people work together in such a way that they pool their initiative and expertise, the outcome is a product or energy which is greater than the sum of their individual actions'.
- Leadership is wider than those appointed to formal leader roles and so there is an 'openness of the boundaries of leadership'.
- Leadership boundaries are open by embracing a range of knowledge and skills so that 'varieties of expertise are distributed across the many, not the few' (p. 7).

Consequently, we have to look beyond the functions of tasks, knowledge and skills of a role-incumbent towards the location and exercise of power, and so what is distributed is not just the technical aspects but possibly the authority, responsibility, and hence legitimacy, to do or not do the work, and the very act or process of distribution is dependent on power sources and interactions. Currently distributed leadership is being characterized as:

- authorized
- dispersed
- democratic

Distributed leadership as *authorized* is where work is distributed from the headteacher to others. This distribution is usually accepted because it is regarded as legitimate through the complex operation of both hierarchy in the form of subordination and through attribution in the form of giving status to a person to determine activity and take actions. In a system is it is through delegation of the leader to the led; in a market it is the empowerment of the led to work in particular ways. Delegation and empowerment are part of the same top-down initiation and flow: delegation puts the interests of the public good above that of the private (i.e. you are doing this because it will make learning improve for all); and empowerment puts the interests of the private above that of the public (i.e. you are doing this to respond to the needs of that individual student). Both are ways of influencing the teacher to do things in ways that are acceptable because they are rationalized as a part of the job, or are about developing the job (and the organization) or the person (promotion), or about achieving reform with new work to do or the traditional work of superiors is delegated to free them up to do new work. When teachers are empowered then it means they are licensed to deliver in ways that recognize some discretion as long as the overall goals are achieved or exceeded. Devolution through giving authentic authority to make decisions with the possibility of some autonomy and consequent challenge to the centre remains an option, but it is unlikely in the current context that a school, even an officially acclaimed successful one, could risk such pluralism.

The implications for Leading Teachers is that leadership remains organizational in both form and function, and it is dependent on the will and skill of formal leaders either to recognize the potential of teachers to lead, or on the experience of overload, to necessitate pushing work down the line. It is a form of leading, one that might be a feature of trying to shift the culture and practice within an organization, but it is not a very dynamic or necessarily productive one in regard to sustained activity.

Distributed leadership as *dispersed* is where much of the work goes on in organizations without the formal working of a hierarchy. Lingard *et al.* (2003, p. 54) endorse how from Australian women's hockey we might characterize this as the 'leaderful team, as a way to reject the "social loafing" which leaves responsibility for achieving outcomes to others'. This distribution is accepted through the legitimacy of the differentiated knowledge and skills of those who do the work. It is more bottom-up through networks in which the private interests of the individual are promoted through group and/or collective actions, and through the community where the public good secures the defence of the individual. In a network it is through the pursuit of interests; and in a community it is through consensus-building around beliefs. Both the pursuit of interests and consensus-building are part of the same bottom-up initiation and flow. The pursuit of interests puts the individual above that of the collective or 'I will do this because it makes sense to me and what matters to me'; and consensus-building puts the collective above that of the individual or 'I will do this because I need to work with others'. Both are ways in which the teacher is recognized as influential through promoting the self as individual and/or through the collective.

One way in which this is being developed is through the argument that much of what goes on in organizations cannot be directly attributed to the impact of leaders (Jermier and Kerr 1997). Gronn (2000) articulates the factors cited regarding this: 'the personal attributes of organization members (e.g. their self-motivation to perform), organizational processes (e.g. autonomous work group norms) and characteristics inherent in the work itself (e.g. its routine or pro-grammed nature)' (p. 319). People getting on with the work and developing that work can be seen as a substitute for leadership if we regard leadership as what role incumbents do to others or leaders as the 'causal agents of work outcomes' (Gronn 2003a, p. 278). If we shift our gaze in the direction that Gronn suggests towards the 'totality of the work that is to be performed by the organization' and examine 'what is required as part of that organization's totality of work prac-tices (in order) to accomplish that body of work' (p. 278), then we can get beneath the relationships that are created and recreated within the organization, and begin to understand the influence flows underlying work processes. Consequently, there are no substitutes for leadership, only leadership, and it is leadership that is practised by others other than the headteacher and formal leaders.

Once the analysis shifts from the leader towards practice then we can engage with distribution from the perspective of the embeddedness of the agent as 'distributed cognition' (Lakomski 2002, p. 1) through to prac-tice conceptualized as 'parallel leadership', where others in addition to the headteacher lead (Crowther 2002, p. 169). A more diffuse approach is to conceptualize distributed leadership as '*stretched over* the school's social and situational contexts' (Spillane *et al.* 2003, p. 535 [authors' emphasis]), and this leads us onto more productive territory where we can examine how and why people work together as distributed practice. Gronn (2000, 2002, 2003a,b,c) has theorized *concertive action* which is more than a numerical aggregation of 'more hands make light work' and instead conceptualizes distribution around 'spontaneity', 'intuitive under-standing' and the existence of 'a variety of structural relations' (Gronn 2002, p. 429).

Spontaneous collaboration gives recognition to leadership within interactions, and people can engage in 'concertively aligned conduct' through anticipated or unanticipated activity that needs intervention and possible problem resolution. Gronn goes on to state:

> One way is when sets of two or three individuals with differing skills and abilities, perhaps from across different organizational levels, pool their expertise and regularise their conduct to solve a problem, after which they may disband. These occasions provide opportunities for brief bursts of synergy which may be the extent of the engagement or the trigger for ongoing collaboration. (Gronn 2002, p. 430)

Working together over time means that people get to know, rely on and trust each other, and Gronn identifies such partnerships as 'co-leaders' who know themselves and are known by others as engaging in leadership: 'Intuitive working relations are analogous to intimate interpersonal relations (e.g. successful marriages and friendships), and two or more members act as a joint working unit within an implicit framework of understanding' (p. 430).

While formal structures exist with role incumbents and job descriptions, the realities of practice means that people may work together in ways that work best, and so there is a difference between the paper-based organizational chart and what actually happens. Gronn (2002, pp. 430–31) talks about 'institutionalised practices' when 'concertively acting units' are attributed as doing leadership, and indeed, 'new elements may be grafted onto existing arrangements or managers may try to regularise informal relations'.

What Gronn (2002) has presented us with is a gradation from the looseness of spontaneity through to the solidity of organization, but central to this is 'conjoint agency' which means: 'that agents synchronise their actions by having regard to their own plans, those of their peers, and their sense of unit membership' (p. 431). For this to happen there needs to be first, 'synergy', where each 'releases' something from each other; and second, 'reciprocal influence', where power is exercised over each other (p. 431). Synergy can be understood through examining boundaries, and two contrasting ones are first, the interrelationship between a senior management team and the middle leadership in a school where the aim is to negotiate through the boundaries in order to align work and goals; and second, a separation of powers where pluralism means that power over and to is not concentrated but rather located in different parts of the organization, so that no one part is able to control absolutely. Both of these have their strengths and problems, and Gronn goes on to argue that if we are to describe (and possibly prescribe) practice, then responsibilities may overlap or be complementary, and so we need to understand how both 'interdependence' and 'coordination' in working relationships is conducted. This allows for specialization and unification in the division of work, proximity and distance in the location of work, and individual and collective involvement in doing work. In other words, we each have a contribution to make, but at some point this has to be worked into a unified whole: we may do our work in the same building or many miles away, and we may do it alone or with others. Such processes are about the use and production of knowledge, and Spillane *et al.* (2001), drawing on

Wenger's work on communities of practice, enable us to capture how distribution is also about cognition:

> Knowledge, understandings, and meanings, gradually emerge through interaction and become distributed among those interacting rather than individually constructed or possessed ... [and so] ... conceptualizing schools as communities of practice, knowledge is viewed as part of a shared repertoire at the disposal of community members ... who engage in joint enterprise. (p. 6)

This certainly gives us a different perspective than that of the 'egg-carton structure' (Spillane *et al.* 2004, p. 53) of division without reintegration, and it certainly comes closer to Leading Teachers as teachers in real time, real life situations because it begins with practice and so challenges the traditional models of 'follower-dependence' in favour of 'interdependence' (Gronn 2003c). Indeed, Harris (2004) is right to alert us to the lack of empirical evidence regarding student outcomes in supporting the case for distribution, and in working for this the field needs to interconnect with what we know about teachers and how their practice develops.

Revealing distributed leadership within practice enables us to ask questions regarding purposes, particularly when set within the context of educational change and the modernization of the school workforce. Gronn (2003b,c) juxtaposes distribution with the intensification of work, and so is able to ask questions about connections with 'greedy work' (2003b, p. 147). Asking or telling someone to participate in a meeting that they haven't been to before, or involving them through asking them to read and give their views on a policy document, or circulating emails to people is actually creating more work. Rarely are people asked or told not to do something in favour of doing something else; at most they postpone it (usually by putting it in their bag to take home) and so distributed leadership could be additive. While work may be exhausting it can also be exhilarating, and so distributed leadership could be addictive (Gronn 2003b: 152). Piling on work and accepting work is not just a feature of psychological or organizational dysfunction, but is how public-sector change is taking place through new work, new people, new relationships combined with the age-old practice of forcing people (in benign and malign ways) to get the job done (Gunter 2001). This makes the need for a politics of practice which simultaneously supports and challenges work all the more vital for the education workforce.

Distributed leadership, in the form of authorized and dispersed leadership, enables us to describe, and hence from this we can develop more sophisticated research strategies, not least because we can reveal the underlying assumptions about power by those who are framing and doing the research. However, Woods (2004, p. 8) argues that 'although leadership may be distributed, it does not necessarily imply an absence of hierarchy', and so we need to be mindful that the debate about distribution is around where the interface is between control and autonomy. Activity is always prescribed, albeit to varying degrees, but limited nevertheless to sustaining the system, the market, the community or the network, and making it work better. Consequently, we should not confuse distributed leadership with democratic leadership, and while the two have some common features, such as the potential for concertive action, there are important distinctive features that need to be articulated and engaged with.

Woods (2004) argues that *democratic* leadership is distinct from distributed leadership in a number of ways:

- While both enable analytical description it is democratic leadership that has more normative potential.
- While both are emergent and reveal dispersal of influence it is democratic leadership that acknowledges formal leaders as well as leadership.
- While both are inclusive it is democratic leadership that has open boundaries, and so involvement is based less on organizational requirements and more on wider and widening recognition.
- While both recognize the importance of the position of those who are in receipt of distribution it is democratic leadership that recognizes the significance and value of dissent, whereas distribution assumes political neutrality.
- While both value autonomy it is democratic leadership that extends this beyond the instrumentality of organizational goals to encompass the rationality of decision making (who has the right and should be given the right to be involved) and ethics (how the pursuit for the truth, the desire for truth, and participation in these matters is conducted and widened).
- While both respect human capacities to be involved it is democratic leadership that extends this beyond the value put on functions towards recognizing, engaging and reintegrating all as a common and public good.

Following on from this analysis we can recognize that we may hold and exercise power to and over and with others, but also we are doing it *for* something. We are seeking the means to recover the teacher as both the alienated worker who is turned off through the instrumentality of delivery and the seduced worker who is turned off through the exhilaration of commitment. Democratic leadership opens up possibilities for Leading Teachers because it widens their gaze from the school as an organization to the wider role of the school as a public institution within a democracy. Teachers and students who are involved in problem-posing and resolution can learn democratic practice, and how to extend democratic opportunities to others (Woods 2004). Furthermore, a respect for security combined with challenging stability can be fostered as being core to how we think about and risk change privately and publicly (Glickman 2002). As democracy is contested within practice then we work for it and struggle over it within context, and as such schools are one place where this takes place and so we can renew it through our planned and unplanned encounters (Reid 2002). Democratic leadership comes closest to how we conceptualize Leading Teachers as more than deliverers of externally determined change to the wider and deeper traditions in our field that encompass how meaning is developed, how experiences are understood and how we work for change.

Moving these arguments forward will be interesting to say the least. England is not yet a mature or authentic democracy but a constitutional monarchy. Concessions have been made that can be characterized as limitations on the traditional in favour of more rational forms of legitimacy. Schools are illustrations of this – hierarchy and the primacy of the headteacher remains (and it could be argued strengthened) with the concession that appointments are based on open competition and credentials rather than birth and nepotism. Wider social barriers regarding class, ethnicity, age and sexuality have been and are being questioned, but still remain strong, and as such are barriers to a wider democratization of educational structures. While democratic forms of leadership are compelling, the danger lies in the label being appropriated to justify organizational makeovers claiming to have democratic credentials. There are some further arguments that need to be addressed by returning to the current drive towards community structures and processes.

Communities at work

How and why we work together, and how we might work together better, are issues underpinning the discussions about distributed leadership. The organizational arrangements to enable working together have focused on teams underpinned by shifts in cultural norms and practices around collaboration and collegiality. I have provided a more detailed analysis of this in *Leaders and Leadership in Education* (Gunter 2001), and in reprising the argument we need to see collaboration and collegiality as distinct. Drawing on Fielding (1999) I would agree that collaboration is functional and organizational, with individuals working together to get the job done; whereas collegiality is social and socializing through a politics of practice. The former is individual and the latter communal; the former is about the instrumentality of resources (acquiring, deploying, evaluating) and the latter is radical in its orientation towards the active use of democratic practices. Neither directing people nor creating the conditions in which either form of working together seems to be achieving the type of control that headteachers need in order to meet the requirements of external agencies. At the same time it does not seem to satisfy the pull towards more participatory models because when grafted onto schools as systems or markets then collaboration can get particular work done; while collegiality is often mere rhetoric because it is too risky in practice. The means of overcoming this is through the current emphasis on how we know and how we might know better through working together.

In education the concept of community has created new insights through which the boundary of the school is less about physical things such as the school gate and more about a local commitment to and trust in beliefs and moral purpose. Sergiovanni (2001), p. 61 argues for 'communities of responsibility', and so

> ... it is norms, values, beliefs, purposes, goals, standards, hopes, and dreams that provide the ideas for a morally based leadership. These ideas are not mandated scripts that require carbon-copy conformity. They are, instead, more like frameworks that function as compasses which provide people with a heightened sense of understanding, meaning, and significance. As a result, plenty of room exists for diversity to be expressed and celebrated in the life of the school ... When leadership is morally based, its effect on spirit, commitment, and results is not only strong but obligatory, allowing the school to function as a community of responsibility. (p. 62)

Diversity is enabled through 'bonding and bridging' (p. 66) or exclusion and inclusion so that connections are made inside and outside the school, and what holds a diverse community together is what is held in common. Through 'altruistic love' (p. 69) the individual can protect the self by beliefs: 'sharing a common framework of values themed to trusting relationships and the development of a culture of respect in schools allows for bringing together a commitment to the common good and individual expression' (p. 70). This requires an approach to leadership that Sergiovanni (2001) calls 'leadership density' which 'refers to the extent leadership responsibilities and practices are located deep among the faculty':

> The more people that are involved in leadership roles and responsibilities, the more dense is leadership in the schools. High leadership density increases the number of people who are engaged in the work of others, the number of people who are responsible for and engaged in the work of others, and thereby augments perception. High leadership density increases the number of people who are trusted with information and thereby enlarges memory. High leadership density increases the number of people concerned with decision making and this augments reason. High leadership density increases the number of people who are exposed to new ideas and thus are more likely to generate even more ideas, thereby enlarging imagination. And, finally, high leadership density increases the number of people who have an important stake in the school and its successes, which augments motivation. (pp. 112–16)

This approach to school leadership is consistent with that being promoted by the NCSL in England as one of the ten propositions that 'taken together they constitute the parameters for a framework for school leadership that is firmly grounded in learning as well as transformational' (Hopkins 2001, p. 8). Proposition 5 states: 'School leadership is a function that needs to be distributed throughout the school community', and so the approach is 'not hierarchical, but federal'. Rejecting the traditional structures within the system, building on the flexibility of the market and preventing dissent (either negative or positive) within networks, the model of leadership being promoted to schools retains the primacy of the headteacher and the structures that sustain this, but it has been overlain by communitarian optimism, and so the emphasis is less on line-management and direction and more on orchestration and performativity:

> This approach to leadership involves building an evolving consensus around values that will unite and excite members of the school community. It means moving the lowest common denominator of school aims to the highest common factor of shared beliefs. It incorporates being articulate about these beliefs and holding action accountable to them – by those leading at all levels. (Hopkins, 2001, p. 11)

The focus on what Gronn (2003d, p. 29) calls 'lateral work formations' has the potential to explore the existence of concertive action with opportunities for democratic leadership. As Harris and Chapman (2002, p. 11) show, 'establishing an "interconnectedness of home, school and community"' and building 'social trust' has been vital for schools facing challenging circumstances. Furthermore, direct links are being made between teacher leadership, distributed leadership and the building of a 'professional learning community ... where teachers participate in leadership activities and decision-making' (Muijs and Harris 2003, p. 440). In times of change the commitment to build a common identity around a shared purpose is a very seductive strategy. However, we would be right to be wary, because trying to settle what holds us in common does have dangers. As Gronn (2003d, p. 30) argues: 'a community of practice does not have an exclusive claim on the allegiance of its members', and so there could be 'rival communities of interest' (30) that could clash, and what counts as a community as distinct from a network or association is difficult to establish given the fluidity of lives. It could be argued that in trying to make a community a unit of analysis then we are both stabilizing and drawing boundaries, and as such we are creating an autarchy that through compliance could have sinister overtones. Indeed, we could argue that the unifying tendency in communitarian approaches means that particular types of knowing are valued compared with others and can be measured against the purposes and expertise of the community, and as such we not only approve of knowing and knowledge but we also deny the power relations that underpin decisions about what is and is not worth knowing. As Contu and Willmott (2000) argue, this means that we don't move from questions of the truth to those of ethics, and if we are to do critical work that strives for change then we need to shift from objective truths to understandings.

Formalizing aspects of people's lives in such a way can mean that our soul is won by others or the desire for survival means that we could present ourselves as such. This all sounds very familiar because history shows that it is the means by which totalitarian regimes secure obedience, and hence we need to wonder what happens when there is dissent with the underlying principles on which the community is based. Indeed, Harber and Davies (2003) ask us to imagine a terrorist training camp as an educational institution, and on the key indicators of leadership effectiveness it would score highly on delivering vision and mission in the production of terrorists. We also need to flip the coin over and look at it from the other side, and recognize that where tyrants have controlled states then those who have overthrown the regime as freedom-fighters have been based in such training camps. In a relatively stable industrialized country such as England then our worries are about performativity, which is toxic for ourselves and for the workplace, but in other parts of the world (this may be closer to home than we might want to admit) we need to give recognition to endemic violence and economic dislocation which is life-threatening.

Harber and Davies (2003) ask: how do we educate street children? How do we educate children orphaned through AIDs? How do we educate children after civil war and genocide? How do we educate children who have learned to hate their neighbour? Perhaps we can learn from this, and as Harber and Davies (2003, p. 142) argue, we need to adopt the principle from the medical profession 'to do no harm' and so instead of the unrelenting drive to improve standards our approach should be about 'lowering distress'. In other words, Harber and Davies (2003) are asking us to think about the values that underpin organizational goals and practices, and the challenge they present is how to enable local context to shape work combined with universal claims to democratic principles. Instead of decentring the leader by focusing on others' leadership, we might remove hierarchy altogether and learn from other parts of the world about more authentic democratic practice through student involvement in decision making; electing headteachers; and schools without headteachers (Davies 1995; MacBeath 1998). Enriching this is Court's (2003) work on sharing leadership without a headteacher, and so Leading Teachers is when teachers collectively lead teaching and learning through collective responsibility. Sustaining this over time is a challenge, but outcomes in the formation of democratic cultures and practices could make its pursuit worthwhile.

If we are really serious about schooling within communities, and if, as Ranson (2000, p. 273) argues, democracy has been 'at a distance from the communities which it was created to serve', then we need to begin with the productive messiness that exists inside and outside our own front doors. The trend toward community is a valuable one for the field to pursue, but the pressure that exists to settle and stabilize practice without ongoing dialogue about power means that we could be working for schools as very sophisticated theme parks. Here there is no place for strangers or for strangeness that challenges our world and with whom we engage with to generate understandings. Everything that is known, worth knowing and should be known is transparent, and so we communicate as a scripted process. I would want to argue for a different approach to this type of fabricated unity:

> ... the most promising kind of unity is one which is *achieved*, and achieved daily anew, by confrontation, debate, negotiation and compromise between values, preferences and chosen ways of life and self-identifications of many and different, but always self-determining, members of the *polis*. This is, essentially the *republican* model of unity, of an emergent unity which is a

joint achievement of the agents engaged in self-identification pursuits, a unity which is an outcome, not an *a priori* given condition, of shared life, a unity put together through negotiation and reconciliation, not the denial, stifling or smothering of differences. (Bauman 2000, p. 178)

Hence I remain restless regarding what the field has so far established about community, distribution and knowledge production, and I would want to take this forward in Chapter 4 by arguing that in order to recover and develop democracy within and for our schools then we need to acknowledge and work for educational leadership as a social practice.

4 Leading Teachers as Researchers

If Leading Teachers is about access to a range of knowledge and knowing, and it is about working within current organizational constraints while working for democratic renewal, then it is through educational research that the interplay between the two is worked through. Leading Teachers are knowers through their practice and by engaging with others who know about practice. Others can be students, colleagues, wider community and professional researchers. Such knowing can be in the library, in experiences, on the internet and can be revealed through personal reflexivity and social interactions. In this chapter I intend to examine the purposes and practices of educational research, and make the case for conceptually informed practice. I argue that we need to shift our focus away from controlling ideas as manageable evidence towards the use and production of ideas. It is through the interplay between the agency of the researcher and the structuring of contextual research that educational leadership as a social practice is experienced and makes a difference.

Knowing research

Teachers (and students) as researchers are on my agenda not as a claim to a new idea, or as recycled ideas, or as a means of undermining researchers who do research as their prime activity. Leading Teachers as researching professionals has a long and vibrant history both through practice and within structured enquiry. What is of concern is how teachers have been pawns in New Right and New Left attempts to undermine professional researchers. While official support for teacher research has been welcomed in the form of funding and renewing the climate for enquiry, it has been based more on arguments about weakness than about enabling educational leadership. In other words, the emphasis has been on the failure of professional researchers to work with teachers as users of research, rather than on revealing and supporting the long-established partnership between higher education and schools, particularly in the field of educational leadership. Indeed, educational research has been criticized for not having a direct impact on practice, and this judgement is a product of linear analysis of focusing on a piece of research and examining a cause-and-effect connection with practice. Ribbins *et al.* (2003) have examined the Australian reviews of educational research, and their comparative analysis with England shows that it is how a review is done that matters. The outcomes in Australia have been more positive not least because the focus has been on 'using more sophisticated methodologies, which work backward from practice', and so 'many of the ways research contributes to practice can be unravelled' (Bates 2002, p. 5). Hence, instead of isolating variables and attempting to measure them we should begin with practice and examine how research is being used in real time, real life activity and actions, within the context of what teachers as researchers are able to do and want to do.

Watkins and Mortimore (1999, p. 12) argue that researching professionals are concerned with 'high complexity within situation' in order to generate short-term actions, while professional researchers focus on 'high complexity across situations' in order to generate 'long-term indirect action'. While scope, orientation and purposes can be different they do complement each other, not least because professional researchers in education are usually practitioners in their own classrooms, and undertaking higher degrees means that researching professionals can do research in other classrooms and schools. Hence the distinction is not necessarily in regard to research aims but rather between proximity and distance from the research site, or between being on the inside or outside. Watkins and Mortimore (1999) go on to argue that

> In our experience, teachers welcome collaboration with people who will work as hard to understand classroom events as the teachers do to conduct them. This demands recognition that teachers possess important expertise and that professional learning is an adaptive process. This process is long term and is critically influenced by contextual factors in the school and local area. At its best, professional development helps teachers to understand their school and to contribute to school-based improvement efforts. In such undertakings the researcher can help the professional to enhance their own knowledge-generation capacities. (p. 13)

The purposes of educational research conducted on the inside and outside by Leading Teachers is central to learning both as a process and as an outcome. We need large-scale longitudinal research that is able to provide general understandings, but we also need small-scale case study work that is about relatability where 'practitioners can relate the context of the case to their own situation' (Bassey 1996, p. 20). What we learn from educational research has become a matter of controversy, not least as Ranson (1998) identifies is the tension between researching to directly impact on practice and on ideas. Ranson (1998) rightly argues that the two are not necessarily separate:

> Knowledge and practice cannot be opposed but only mutually reinforcing. Practice without understanding of the enduring forms of knowledge is blind, while knowledge detached from the world of practice remains impotent and pointless. The learning process is not a 'technical competence' and cannot unfold without a recognition that knowledge is explored through, but also created in, reflective practice. (p. 50)

If Leading Teachers are knowers and can in partnership with others reveal and develop wider and deeper knowing then how does this look in practice? Like many Schools of Education throughout the country the University of Birmingham has a long history of working with teachers as educational leaders through research. For my own part I have been working with teachers in masters and doctoral work and in the following vignettes I will provide illustrations of knowledge (what is known), knowing (how knowing is known) and knowers (how a range of people know) within educational leadership.

Knowing through research

Gail Bagnall is an advanced skills teacher in a Birmingham school, and a member of the Thinking Skills Fellowship devised in association with the University of the First Age (UFA). Gail is interested in the development of thinking skills across the curriculum in order to support responsible and self-directed learning. Her starting point was to examine research evidence on thinking skills and she adopted the McGuinness (1999) typology: (1) generic approaches (e.g. de Bono); (2) subject-specific approaches (e.g. cognitive acceleration in maths education); (3) and infusion approaches (e.g. accelerated learning). She then undertook an action research project based on staff-development needs, inservice sessions and examining the impact of this learning on attitudes and practice. The outcome of the work is summarized in Bagnall (2002):

> ... I feel that staff are now ready to move forward with thinking skills ... There is already planning taking place to incorporate brain-based learning into the tutorial programme ... All the staff I talked to want the students to become independent learners to prepare them for life-long learning. They will be learning about their strengths and hopefully work at developing the weaker areas. There are obviously some staff that are still very sceptical but there are enough to move forward and hopefully the others will see what is happening and want to come on board. The meeting that I held

> with other staff illustrated that there has already been a lot of work carried
> out to develop thinking skills. Unfortunately departments were not aware
> of what was happening in other areas. There is a need for more sharing of
> good practice to go on in school. I feel there is a place for more observation
> of colleagues within other teaching areas to be arranged. (p. 12)

The head and senior management support this initiative, and Gail Bagnall
is intending to build on this work through a sabbatical that will support
her action research through innovations in professional development
and visits to other schools to examine how they have worked on these
matters.

Toby Close is a senior manager in a Birmingham school who undertook a study of middle management in a secondary school as part of his
doctoral programme, 'Leaders and Leadership in Education'. He began
by reading the literature on middle management in schools, and his
critical synthesis of this work produced a model regarding role:

- The *negotiator role*: 'This encompasses the brokering function,
  translating policies from above and below, ensuring their implementation and representing the department ...'
- The *empowerment* role: 'This describes approaches to leadership
  that foster collegiality and the achievement of joint goals ...'
- The *leading professional* role: 'This explains the head of department
  role as "leading from the front" as an exemplar of best practice,
  supporting staff and providing up-to-date innovation and continuous professional development to develop effective teaching and
  learning.' (Close 2003, p. 4)

Close completed a case-study of middle management in a secondary
school through a focus group of nine middle managers (four heads of
department and three heads of year). The outcome of this work showed
that through brokering activity those in the middle were striving to create
a meaningful role for themselves between teachers and senior managers.
In time of change it is teachers in formal organizational roles working in
the middle that make things happen in day-to-day practice. Linked to this
is how empowerment is defined by practitioners as working together to
challenge practice and generate new ideas. Nevertheless, these teachers
did lead from the front as practitioners in teaching and learning, and
in coaching and supporting other teachers. While the three roles are
helpful in illuminating practice, they also uncover complexities within
that practice, and in particular the tensions between delivering in the
middle and at whole-school level. They note that their goals in the middle
matter, and that they 'selectively apply and ignore directives from above'

(Close 2003, p. 10) to enable this. Furthermore, the research shows two important areas that need further work: (1) how those who work in the middle have a high contact load but also a high degree of responsibility and accountability for other teachers' work; and (2) there are contextual issues regarding the type of middle role (e.g. academic, pastoral and the size and history of the department or team). Close concludes that more work is needed on the biographies and experiences of those who work in the middle, so that we have more fine-grained descriptions both of their work and how it is located within the complexity of practice.

Alan Kirsz is a teacher in Birmingham who undertook a study of the effectiveness of a geography department in a secondary school as a part of his doctoral programme, 'Leaders and Leadership in Education'. Through undertaking a critical review of school effectiveness research, and focusing on the work on departmental effectiveness, he designed a study based on capturing pupil perceptions of effectiveness. This is a small-scale study for a module assignment, and he designed a questionnaire containing questions regarding lesson preparation, pupil participation, assessment and the learning environment that was administered to a 10 per cent sample from Years 7–10. He found a variation in the views of pupils of different abilities, 'with the more able pupils regarding teaching and learning to be more effective than less able pupils. The most noticeable difference is in their views about questions relating to assessment, where the less able view the department less favourably' (Kirsz 2002, p. 15). He goes on to argue that

> The findings have implications for the leadership of the department. It has been argued that school and subject leadership impacts on teaching and learning and that pupils have a valuable role to play in informing on the effectiveness. Since theirs are not the only voices that should be heard, the following comments are expressed in the conditional ... it could be that the subject leader needs to focus more on the teaching and learning in the department; particularly those areas identified as 'underperforming'. This could mean developing many of the characteristics of instructional leadership; albeit at middle management level. This may involve fostering a greater common sense of purpose, creating more opportunities for staff to share and develop ideas and practice, providing more informed feedback to staff as a result of monitoring with a teaching and learning focus and challenging staff to interrogate their practices in the classroom. The ramifications of this may be that the subject leader will need to affect a change in culture. (p. 16)

An important outcome of this work is the judgement that school effectiveness research needs to examine the underlying epistemology regarding cause-and-effect connections, and once we acknowledge the role of teachers and students who have agency then it is difficult to measure the impact of abstracted school and departmental effects on this.

Marie-Thérèse Rollins is a teacher and middle manager, and through her Masters studies, 'Management for Learning', she undertook an action-research project into homework. In particular, she is interested in the low completion rate for homework, the impact on progress and how the homework policy and practice might be improved. Building on theories of change, Rollins began with gathering teacher, pupil and parent attitudes to homework, before working with other staff and pupils as fellow researchers to make interventions in practice and to monitor activity. The outcomes have been positive:

> As far as the school as an organization is concerned the project could be seen as having had quite an impact. From the new academic year the school day will be changed to allow for a tutorial period at the end of the day, thus giving an opportunity to begin work on homework and seek support from tutors. In addition, the need to provide after-school facilities for our students is seen as important; the sessions will begin in the new term and will be linked to an incentive scheme which we hope will encourage pupils to take advantage of school resources. The fact that funding has been provided to support further this project is a step forward and will help to make current achievements in this domain sustainable. It is too early to judge upon the impact on pupils' performance, although as previously mentioned teachers' responses to homework could be said to be having a noticeable impact. The proposed innovations in rewards and sanctions will be the object of a close monitoring exercise, and it is hoped that it will bring qualitative data to continue the review cycle. (Rollins 2002, p. 22)

In telling the story of this research and how it unfolded, wider issues of competing priorities and the politics of prioritizing came to the fore. The realities of having to handle whole-school strategy with what pupils regarded as barriers to homework completion combined with teacher practice in the design and follow-up on homework, is the terrain in which her research was located. Rollins notes that she has learned that acknowledging complexity through including pupils is worthwhile because it has strengthened trust and given primacy to voice, and in finding a way through real life situations shows that 'changes occur through a series of negotiations, not through a tightly controlled plan' (Rollins 2002, p. 22).

Sam Smith, as a Birmingham secondary teacher, became a Fellow of the University of the First Age (UFA), and funding by the Paul Hamlyn Foundation meant that she was able to attend every Monday afternoon for two years professional development sessions on innovative ways of approaching teaching and learning. The UFA enables out-of-hours learning through super learning days, Easter and summer schools, and learning sessions after school, e.g. homework clubs. UFA Fellows not only run this activity but also lead inservice sessions for teachers in their school in UFA approaches to learning, and train students as peer mentors to support other students' learning. Integral to the Fellowship was an action-research project where Fellows identified interventions designed to make a difference to teaching and learning. Of particular significance is how this work has been underpinned by Howard Gardner's (1991) work on multiple intelligences, and Smith describes how in collaboration with another colleague they developed 'Buzz your Brain':

> These sessions were geared for Year 11 to prepare them for their exams. It included information about the brain, discovering pupils' multiple intelligences and then discussions on how the memory worked and finally mind-mapping techniques. In our second year (we) ran these *Buzz Your Brain* sessions, but this time based on feedback from the first year. We changed the order and the content so that at every session we always had practical examples of subject material that the students actually needed to know for their exams and a way of learning it. (Smith 2001, p. 9)

This activity has had an impact on Sam Smith, other teachers and the students. She tells us that 'I see myself as a motivator and a communicator. I am interested in helping students to fulfil their potential at school by providing an atmosphere that encourages learning and one that fosters the ownership of their learning' (Smith 2001, pp. 12–13). Central to achieving this has been the development of the Teaching and Learning Committee (TLC), which is 'fondly referred to as the TLC', and

> ... at this forum, the staff can get to grips with teaching and learning issues that are actually affecting us, the teachers at [school]. [name] and myself facilitate this meeting but it is not lead by us. The Teaching and Learning Committee was set up to deal with current issues that occur, now, at our school. It has the remit to broaden the range of teaching and learning strategies that are currently being used by staff. It is a forum by which [name] and I can pass on ideas gathered at the UFA, so that staff can try them for themselves and feedback with improvements, adjustments or any comments that might be applicable to our students. It will be used to trial lessons based on multiple intelligences to see how our students' respond and how lessons can be adopted across subject areas. Then the information can be shared with the whole school via whole-school INSET (inservice training) sessions or department meetings where appropriate. The most important factor is that the lessons and ideas are for our students and are current. (p. 16)

What Smith's action-research project shows is that ideas and theories about learning are vitally important, and combined with local research data regarding practice, together with the establishment of a forum such as the TLC to engage in dialogue about ideas and data, has created a very powerful process. She quotes the headteacher: 'any ideas coming from you will be more readily received by other staff because they are not coming from me' (Smith 2001, p. 49), and this bottom-up perspective on owning developments in professional practice is regarded as inspiring.

These short accounts of teacher research illuminate the vitality of the interplay between practice and ideas. We think we know about our work, but the design and implementation of a research strategy can affirm our knowing and open up new ways of knowing. We can ask our own questions and gain access to questions that others want to ask. We can research what we know from our own practice and from others' practice through planned data collection, dialogue and reading. We can use this data to plan and make interventions in practice in order to explore ideas, undertake feasibility studies, describe situations and engage with change. We can work for change, and not only do democratic things such as including pupils in our work, but also develop democratic opportunities through how we think about and go about designing and conducting our practice. All of this requires intellectual work through engaging with ideas and devising strategies both to get those ideas listened to and acted upon. Furthermore, we can maintain our commitment to caring for students while improving their access to and experiences of learning. Hence leadership is not so much about futuristic visions led by charismatic role incumbents but rather about educational issues that teachers are handling every day in their work with pupils and their colleagues.

Conceptually informed practice

The realities of decisions do not fit the prescriptions or idealized diagrams of plan, implement and evaluate (Gunter 1997). Decision making is about power to and over, and so choices are not really made according to the strictures of a prefabricated scheme but largely through reading the situation. We should not be seduced by the abstract language of rationality used to explain choices, as research evidence shows that while heads may use the required labels expected by outsiders, in reality they do what they have always done and that is to negotiate and do deals (Gronn 1996). Starratt (2003) helps us to understand this further:

Administrators need not surrender to the seeming impossibility of acting rationally and simply follow their own private hunches and beliefs. Educational administration requires a constant effort to introduce rationality into decisions. That rationality does not come exclusively from the individual administrator, but comes more from individuals involved in the decision discussing the merits of alternative choices. Even then, decisions rarely if ever are purely rational; to seek for that kind of rational purity is to chase an unattainable ideal. Rather, what administrators should seek are the most reasonable decisions under the circumstances – decisions for which others can take responsibility because they have been involved in making them. (p. 5)

Here Starratt is using the term 'educational administration' in the way that it is used internationally (and historically in England) to describe policy-making and what we now call educational leadership (Gunter 2004). Involvement in making decisions means that participants have a range of evidence to draw on:

(1) the *experience* of how this issue or related issues have been dealt with before;
(2) an understanding of *context* regarding what the situation is that is being decided about;
(3) the potential *impact* on people and how the decision will be read and lived;
(4) the *research* findings or what we know about this issue from other situations;
(5) our own *theories* and those from the social sciences that can help to describe and explain how we might understand and develop options for the way forward;
(6) *dialogue* or how participants give recognition to and engage with finding a way through the complexity that is real-life, real-time situations.

There are times to be robust and times to back off. There is much that is not known and will never be known, and so we are always working with an uncertain and incomplete sense of knowing. Knowledge and knowing, and our predispositions to reveal this knowing, are embodied. As Bourdieu (1990) argues, we fall into practice as improvisation rather than have our practice necessarily predetermined by structures. This is why our focus should be less on the types of objectified knowledge and knowing, and more on how as agents, on our own and with others, are given access to knowledge, and how we use it and produce it through the choices we make and the actions we take.

Conceptually informed practice is located within reflexivity as a practice. I have argued elsewhere (Gunter 1997) that we have adopted a very shallow and timid form of the reflective practitioner through which we are invited to be cognitively and emotionally intelligent about our practice, and so self-discipline ourselves to fit the preferred model of practice. In much of what is written about this type of reflection we can see how the radicalism has been ripped out to leave behind a hollow process that supports conformity and enables us to feel better about it. In contrast, reflexivity asks the individual and the group to relate their thinking and proposed strategies to the wider context in which they are working, and so rather than try to solve a problem that is not their problem at all, or their problem alone, they are able to ask serious questions about the situation and how to move forward. Reflexivity is more than knowing what to do and doing it, and it is more than having outside expert evidence to back up what you are doing. As Delanty (2001) argues:

> … my conception of reflexivity extends beyond the level of the individual social actor to the expression of crisis in public communication and discourse in which intersubjectively shared assumptions are problematized in open-ended discourses. In this use of the term, which is more constructivist and less self-referential, the reflexive moment refers to the articulation of crisis and social construction by processes that are far from being under the control of any social actor. (p. 154)

The experience within practice of the interplay between agency and structure means that in a site within the field of educational leadership, such as a school, habitus is revealed as a structure, and is itself structured through taking up a position and being positioned. Hence reflexivity is about knowing the rules of the game, and is about staking capital as claims for recognition.

Experiencing conceptually informed practice

I asked teachers to provide some short accounts of their experiences of doing educational research. When I made the invitation to be involved each teacher was given the same guidance but each interpreted it differently. The excitement of teaching is how you learn as a teacher, and the experience of reading such accounts has shown me that this is a metaphor for the whole book and how we need to engage with teachers as dynamic and interesting people.

> **Gail Bagnall** I have completed two pieces of action research and I am currently working on a third. They have made me look at what is happening

in my school and other schools. Until I took on this work I would attend one-day courses, try out ideas that were being suggested but did not look at the effect they may or may not be having on the students. With action research you need to look at the present situation and then carry out some interventions and then look at how these have made a difference.

I still feel very frustrated with my first piece of action research. I started off looking at multiple intelligences and the results of the CAT (Cognitive Abilities Test) tests. I was unable to find a link, but then I went on to explore how the CAT test results were used and made some recommendations. Unfortunately we are still only using these results to look at the predictions for pupils and for calculating value-added results. I am still trying to encourage the team responsible for data that we should also look at possible strategies for particular groups of students.

My second piece of work looked at thinking skills in school and as part of this a Teaching and Learning Group was set up which has had an impact on the members of the group, and this is now spreading out to the rest of the staff. The group has produced many teaching aids.

From the work I am doing now, which continues to look at teaching and learning, and also at continuing professional development, there has been one particular change in school. Staff have been given time within their teams to look at various aspects of teaching and learning and to give their teams opportunities to develop ideas to contribute towards the teaching and learning policy. There has also been time to share how we are incorporating ideas into our teaching.

For my own personal development it has made me look at articles and books related to my action research, making me more aware of recent research into teaching and learning. Having been back in teaching for ten years after a ten-year gap I found it very refreshing to try out new ideas, reject or adapt them if they did not work, and adopt the ones that were effective. I have also passed on information to teachers in school and am always keen to hear ideas from others. I am now more likely to question what is happening in school and what effect changes may have on our students and staff. There are always new ideas being put forward for what is to be taught in school and what records we need to keep. I see action research as a way of looking at the effect of these changes and if they are improving the education of our students.

Toby Close My decision to undertake an education doctorate stemmed from the realization that the increasing number and range of one day INSET opportunities I was being mailed as head of department was doing little to improve my knowledge, skills and understanding as a middle manager (or my waistline). The weakness of these courses lies in their 'one size fits all' approach and the limited scope of the training. In contrast the EdD (Doctor of Education) is a process not an event, offering a personal and professional challenge with the requirement to reflect upon existing practice. As a result, my main reason for undertaking an EdD was the potential, as a practising teacher, to explore current leading-edge models surrounding leaders and leadership and to reflect on and apply them to my own specific school context in order to improve my own practice.

It is crucial that practising teachers are involved in the production of knowledge surrounding education and educational leadership rather than just seen as the receivers of knowledge. The EdD gives teachers the skills and credibility to challenge perceived wisdom about 'what works' in order to capture the complexity of working in schools. This is crucial if teachers are going to meet the needs of their specific school and its community.

I am currently in the second year of my EdD and about to embark on my thesis. In preparation for this, the course has been structured around both research training and a variety of subject modules related to educational leadership. This has equipped me with the necessary skills to examine critically existing literature about all aspects of school leadership and to undertake research pertinent to my position as a senior teacher. For example, I have recently studied the changing role of subject leaders by conducting a focus group of middle managers to learn about their experiences of managing from the middle. I have benefited greatly by undertaking research within my own organization and the insights gained by contrasting theory with the everyday reality in schools and at the chalk-face. Colleagues too have expressed professional satisfaction by examining their roles within the organization. The findings and analysis were fed back to the head in order that she might recognize the opportunities and obstacles these crucial leaders faced.

In my forthcoming thesis I will be examining the factors affecting decisions surrounding whether to apply for promotion to subject leadership, and will pay particular attention to fast-track teachers. This builds upon my previous research undertaken during the course and stems from my interest in career pathways. It also provides an opportunity to investigate issues that have been pertinent to my own career development.

Hilary Dowen The research I undertook was part of a Thinking Skills for Learning Fellowship and involved a study of the work of Edward de Bono with specific reference to his six thinking-hats. I was interested to establish if the thinking-hats and PMI [Plus, Minus, Interesting] tool were transferable to a range of different situations and subjects by the pupils themselves. This interest arose out of my experience as head of a religious education department where evaluation skills accounted for 25 per cent of the GCSE (General Certificate of Secondary Education) examination course. Repeated reports from examination boards emphasized that pupils receive a grade D or lower because they cannot supply evidence of reasoned consideration of two different points of view expressed coherently. Evaluation is a skill that is required in all national curriculum subjects, and so I was keen to find alternative methods to such things as writing-frames that I had used previously. Having followed a broadly philosophical approach to the teaching of RE, I was aware that children could grasp difficult concepts and discuss in detail philosophical questions in Year 7, but by the end of Key Stage 3 were often very one-sided in their views which appeared to harden at Key Stage 4. The techniques that de Bono advocated 'broke the thinking down' and gave a structure to support the development of thinking through various stages and prevented 'knee-jerk' reactions to a problem or debate. This combined with the problem of transferability by pupils themselves across their learning experiences led to my interest in action research. I formed a strategy to consider if de Bono's techniques, while classified as a general approach to thinking, could indeed be transferred to a variety of learning situations. This in turn could be measured in terms of pupil progress and attainment. This work, however, coupled with the demands of a teaching job, can take rather a long time to complete.

The action research process itself has achieved many things in terms of my own personal development:

- Being the instigator and a manager of change. As a research fellow within a school I was able to lead curriculum developments and successfully implement these within a whole-school context. I succeeded in overcoming many sceptics who were often part of the school's senior management team. In terms of career progression this experience should be extremely useful, as progression to senior management requires the ability to initiate and manage change.
- Renewed enthusiasm for my own classroom teaching. Having had some sixteen years experience at the time of beginning the research it was invigorating to encounter new and exciting ways to encourage thinking. While I had always tried to use a variety of different teaching techniques my personal increase in knowledge also led to an increase in confidence to try out different teaching methods.

I was also able to bring on board many other colleagues who were keen to learn with me, and I was able to establish a research and development group where colleagues agreed to try out some of the techniques themselves. This interest was for me quite surprising, since some senior managers had decided that the staff were not ready for such ideas and discussions. I found the opposite to be the case because staff of all ages were keen to improve classroom practice.

Through the action research I was able to exchange ideas and receive support from course participants and tutors. These relationships, once established, can be called upon at any time to discuss ideas relating to learning and research.

For the children's learning, their ability to ask themselves higher-order questions became apparent, along with their reflection on the learning process itself and their own recognition of the need for transferability of their skill development across the curriculum. All pupils out of over 400 were, for instance, able to give examples of subjects where creativity was needed and where the six thinking-hats could be used to aid their learning.

Pupils after a Super Learning day sought me out and talked of their enthusiasm for de Bono. For example, some parents had bought their Year 7 children a de Bono CD on CoRT [Cognitive Research Trust] thinking which they came to discuss with me. In an evaluation of the same day, one pupil wrote that he had learned something that he could use for the rest of his life in and out of school.

For the organization, action research should be part of a school's self-improvement process. It is easier if the research is part of the school's development plan. The school through the research fellow gains access to a wider community of professional experts, and providing the action researcher has the personal skills to be able to overcome sceptics and other obstacles, can be a tremendous catalyst for change and improvement by bringing this knowledge with them and into the school. As such it is also a cheap option for staff development training, providing the senior management make full use of the research and research fellow.

While being thoroughly enjoyable, the most frustrating thing is finding the time for the reading and writing-up process, and the fact that such research must be based on evidence such as the measurement of pupil progress. This can take a long period of time to determine exactly.

Dee Dunne I started my EdD programme in October 1999, following a complete change in my career path. Prior to gaining my first headship in 1985 I had completed an MEd – also at Birmingham University. Although this had been a thoroughly interesting course and useful for me in that it added to my qualifications for headship, it was at the time very theoretical. The EdD degree is research based and allows the students to bring their own professional experiences to their work. The main focus of the work is Leaders and Leadership mainly within educational settings. Working through the research has made me reflect on my own styles of leadership and where I probably went wrong in my attempts to bring about change. The module on Leadership focused on contrasting different contexts and was an amazing experience through observing and interviewing a manager from (name of company) in the carrying out of her duties. The amount of money passing through the store in one 24-hour period was equivalent to the annual budget for a large primary school.

My main study is looking at the changes in primary education since the 1988 Education Reform Act. I have three schools as case-studies and have spent a lot of time interviewing members of staff, studying documents and observing the schools at work. It is tempting to carry on researching and never get down to the writing. The time I have spent in these schools has given me opportunities to reflect on good practice and enabled me to focus especially on styles of leadership. As an ex-head I find myself comparing their styles with mine. Does the gender of the headteacher influence his/her management style? What about the length of time in post?

It is especially liberating to have given myself the time to carry out this research and the time to think about what I am doing. I'm often asked what am I going to do afterwards, but for me the research does not impinge on 'afterwards' – I am doing it for myself. While carrying out my research I am working as a supply teacher and I find myself examining styles of leadership in a covert manner – does that head show transformational leadership? Are the staff agreeing with the head, or are they following their own agenda? It's people-watching with a slant. Intellectually I feel challenged and stretched – being in a position of leadership at a time of rapid change gives only time to cope with events, and there is always the feeling of nothing being completed properly. It is only now while researching and analysing the work of other heads that I can reflect on my own styles and achievements.

As a researcher, I am invited into people's lives, but on their terms, and this has to be reflected in the writing. I have also had to made a conscious effort to stand back when interviewing heads and not be too sympathetic – my research needs to be based on rigour not fellow-feeling. [There is also] the discipline of setting one's own pressures – I am in charge of my own work and not working to someone else's timetable.

For my future, when I have completed my research – I don't know. If I was returning to headship I know I'd be completely different, and not just because I've been away from the scene for a while but because my attitude and approaches have been productively challenged and changed by my research.

Alan Kirsz Why did I respond to the flier on the staff room noticeboard advertising the EdD course and thus become involved in educational research? I suppose I had come to a stage in my life when I wanted a new challenge and the EdD course looked attractive since it had the taught component that would enhance my professional development. The research 'training' modules was also a 'seller' since I felt that this was an important means of support.

Having 'signed up' I was soon told that I was now part of the 'research community'. I had visions of being sucked into some sort of insular sect remote from everyday folk. This was far from the truth. Once I had got over the culture shock of the language used on the course (having realized after many a discussion with fellow novices that the language was not a façade that academics use to hide behind), I soon began to enjoy the course, and in some sort of perverse way I really began to look forward to the gatherings. Had I been successfully socialized into the club and passed the initiation procedures?

Your views and perspectives counted. They were juxtaposed and interpreted alongside the wealth of experience of research of the course staff. There was an intellectual welcome. What really appealed to me was the emphasis on questioning the assumptions of knowledge claims and the 'proclaimed' truths of the establishment. What me, a radical? Was it a mid-life crisis in wishing to revisit my undergraduate days? What dawned on me was that it was important to question these things, especially at a time when the teaching profession was becoming deprofessionalized by successive governments hell-bent on pursuing their own political agendas with limited opportunities provided by them to question their interpretation of what makes good schools, good teaching and good learning. A voice crying in the wilderness? Perhaps.

I doubt that what I have done has consciously affected how I work as a subject-leader and teacher, but then am I in the best position to make such a judgement? What has happened is that I have been intellectually challenged and I feel that I am in a stronger position to question knowledge claims. It is a sort of personal satisfaction, but one I would recommend to all involved in education. It would be wrong of me to pretend that it has not been difficult fitting in the studies alongside the demands made by my family and work. But it has proved possible to do so.

It helps to be able to critique what counts as valid knowledge if you have experienced the knowledge-forming process. The evaluation and a chance to try out a range of methodologies and question their underlying assumptions has been particularly valuable. For if more people felt confident to question the basis of knowledge claims, there might be more resistance to education being used as a political football. I suppose the acid test for me is what I do after I have finished the course. If I continue to question knowledge claims it will be all the more important. If I don't and revert to the easy life of acceptance, then is it horses for courses?

Sam Smith Why would anyone want to do educational research? It's boring, it takes time and effort, it's got edu-babble (like techno-babble), it makes you think and then think some more. Wait! Wait a minute ... it does make you think! I think about the information I have found out ... ooh that's interesting I could use that. Next time I teach 8P I'm gonna do that.

Pants!! That didn't work very well. What did that book say, Ok then, next time I try that (... if I dare) I'm gonna do it like this! Yeah (pumps fist in the air). I did it – gosh that was great! I took that piece of information from the book, from my findings in the study I did, and what an exciting result! The students in 8P loved it, more importantly they understood the concept *and* we made links to other things. I wonder ... will it work with the dreaded 12P?

Sometimes reading those books (about education) is like pulling teeth: I read the paragraph once, didn't understand it, I read it again ... Still don't get it! You know I can understand each individual word, but together they might as well be written in Chinese and (you've guessed it) I'm not fluent in Chinese. Yet I *keep trying* ... eventually the penny will drop and eventually I'll be able to understand the meaning and make use of it.

When I am doing my own research I frequently ask myself what am I doing this for? – I get so frustrated. But I force myself to continue and try and reach the higher meaning, so when I face my students I can make a difference in their education, in their lives.

As a teacher – teacher first, maths teacher second – I feel such a responsibility to get it right. To arm the students we teach with not just the skills required for life – being able to do your taxes, etc. – but the desire to learn. To give students the opportunity to enrich their lives for themselves by giving them the ability to pursue knowledge, if they want to. I know how much I love learning new stuff. I think everybody has the right to get great pleasure from learning.

That's why I force myself on, I want to understand what makes teaching and learning, and in particular the bridge between the two, tick!

These are living accounts of conceptually informed practice in action. We can identify the development and challenge in experiencing agency through understanding practice and how they might engage with that practice. This takes place within context, and as such the structure and culture of the organization and wider networks can interplay with agency: it can enhance and it can stifle. Identities as teacher through knowing and having respect as a knower are developing, and there is an emerging politics of practice around how we can make a difference.

Educational leadership as social practice

The challenge that I have taken up is how to restore meaningful and active agency in education. However, 'leadership-centric' research still dominates, and it is still the case that the most officially preferred work is that of 'studies assuming and producing leadership through designs with inbuilt "proofs" of leadership, carried out by researchers ideologically and commonsensically committed to the idea' (Alvesson and Sveningsson 2003, p. 379). Hence the trend remains that teachers are being remodelled as organizational leaders where they lead on tasks and processes to generate unity not only within the school but also within the wider community. It seems that we are experiencing fabricated agency rather than authenticating it. The school in partnership or federation with other schools may no longer be a part of a gated community fearful of the competitive environment, but in shifting the boundary to embrace others through so-called shared visions then we are in danger of limiting rather than generating educational leadership.

Looking at teaching and learning from another vantage point helps us to see that knowledge is not primarily an object to be known and measured but rather a distributed and hence social practice. If we begin by understanding the agency of practitioners and the structure of practices, and how the two are not binaries or dualities but interplay with each other, then we can begin both to describe and understand activity and actions. A good starting point is to look at Wenger's work (Lave and Wenger 1991; Wenger 1998, p. 2000; Wenger and Snyder 2000) that has become a very popular resource for the field to draw on (Bennett and Anderson 2003; Gronn 2003d). However, we do need to heed O'Neill's (2003, p. 154) warning that the field could be in danger of continuing its practice of being 'intellectual camp-followers' through picking up and using such work in an uncritical way. Wenger and Snyder (2000, p. 139) characterized communities of practice as 'groups of people informally bound together by shared expertise and passion for joint enterprise'. These communities connect in a range of ways through meetings and emails. Connections can be structured through agendas or are spontaneous: 'people in communities of practice share their experiences and knowledge in free-flowing, creative ways that foster new approaches to problems' (p. 140). This approach to self-organization around interests and expertise, driven by passion and commitment, has grown out of engagement with chaos theory and the challenge it created for how we interplay knowledge and organizing (Gunter 1997). In particular, while there are boundaries to the community they are created through 'shared practice' (Wenger 2000, p. 232) and through processes that both bridge and interact with others.

What Wenger's (2000, p. 227) theorizing within communities of practice can do is to situate agency through the construction of a 'social learning system' where we identify ourselves as knowing through competence and experience: 'the *competence* that our communities have established over time (i.e. what it takes to act and be recognized as a competent member), and our ongoing *experience* of the world as a member (in the context of a given community and beyond)'. We belong to a community of practice through engagement (doing and talking), imagination (building images of ourselves and the world) and alignment (coordinating activities). Through 'designing itself' (p. 230), e.g. events, leadership, connectivity, membership, learning projects and artefacts (pp. 231–2) a community of practice uses 'learning energy', 'mutuality' and 'a degree of self-awareness' about the 'repertoire that it is developing and its effects on its practice' (p. 230). Through 'shared practice' boundaries are created, and it is within and on the edge of boundaries that learning takes place:

> At the boundaries, competence and experience tend to diverge: a boundary interaction is usually an experience of being exposed to a foreign competence. Such reconfigurations of the relation between competence and experience are an important aspect of learning. If competence and experience are too close, if they always match, not much learning is likely to take place. There are no challenges; the community is losing its dynamism and the practice is in danger of becoming stale. Conversely, if experience and competence are too disconnected, if the distance is too great, not much learning is likely to take place either. (p. 233)

While a community of practice is a unified and stabilizing learning relationship it interconnects with other 'subcommunities' in ways that are integrative. Potential conflicts at boundary margins are recognized through the vitality of brokers who are 'roamers' in making connections and communicating news. Ultimately while the business organization must compete, those within communities of practice must not:

> In these learning systems, organizations find the talents they need, new ideas, technological developments, best practices, and learning partners. The rules of participation in social learning systems are different from those of product markets. You don't simply compete; in fact, your most threatening competitor may be your best partner when it comes to learning together. If you hoard your knowledge in a social learning system, you quickly appear as taking more than you give, and you will progressively be excluded from the most significant exchanges. In a knowledge economy, sustained success for any organization will depend not only on effective participation in economic markets, but, just as importantly and with many of the same players, on knowing how to participate in broader social learning systems. (Wenger 2000, pp. 244–5)

Working to create spaces for stability so that managers can manage in a fluid and rapidly changing world is the enduring feature of private-sector organization theory, and as such it is a useful location for those located within school effectiveness and school improvement. What makes Wenger's work attractive is that it begins with the organization and is concerned with both securing access to the self-motivation and energies of the worker, but in a way that simultaneously promotes and neutralizes agency. The emphasis is on how to improve organizational performance rather than on how to understand and explain social practice. What Wenger's work has in common with school improvement and effectiveness is: (1) an emphasis on process in ways that veil the exercise of power;

(2) a concern for organizational unity at the expense of diversity and working for justice; (3) an approach to knowledge production without dialogic reflexivity.

There is much in common with Bourdieu (we can compare community with field, and identity with habitus), but what Wenger's communities of practice lacks is a rigorous theory of power. Wenger abstracts and fixes the rules of the game, while Bourdieu enables understanding of the rules as they are revealed through practice. Bourdieu's theory of practice enables us to understand and explain practice through the interplay of agency and structure. The question Bourdieu asks is 'how can behaviour be regulated without being the product of obedience to rules?' (Bourdieu 1990, p. 65). Central to Wenger's promotion of identity is how we define ourselves through who we are and who we are not, and where we do and do not belong. He notes that there is a duality to this power where identity 'is the power to belong, to a certain person, to claim a place with the legitimacy of membership' and negotiation is about 'the vulnerability of belonging to, identifying with, and being part of some communities that contribute to defining who we are and thus have a hold on us' (Wenger 1998, p. 207). What is missing here are the structures that structure our identity and how our practice structures those structures. For Bourdieu it is through habitus or our dispositions within practice that reveal structures and become structuring: 'habitus is that presence of the past in the present which makes possible the presence in the present of the forthcoming' (Bourdieu 2000, p. 210). Habitus 'becomes active only *in relation to a field*' (Bourdieu 1990, p. 116) as a place of struggle over position and the staking of capital.

Like Wenger, Bourdieu talks about knowing about who we are, and in his language he talks about 'the sense of the game acquired through prolonged immersion in the game, a sense of positioning ... which always involves a sense of the place of others' (Bourdieu 1990, p. 113). However, Bourdieu enables the interplay between agency and structure to be theorized in ways that prevent the agent as determined by external structures or subjectified as unsocialized cognition:

> It is clear that the problem should not be discussed in terms of spontaneity and constraint, freedom and necessity, individual and society. The habitus as the feel for the game is the social game embodied and turned into second nature. Nothing is simultaneously freer and more constrained than the action of the good player. He quite naturally materializes at just the place the ball is about to fall, as if the ball were in command of him – but by that very fact, he is in command of the ball. The habitus, as society written into the body, into the biological individual, enables the infinite number of acts

of the game – written into the game as possibilities and objective demands – to be produced; the constraints and demands of the game, although they are not restricted to a code of rules, *impose themselves* on those people – and those people alone – who, because they have a feel for the game, a feel, that is, for the immanent necessity of the game, are prepared to perceive them and carry them out. (Bourdieu 1990, p. 63, author's own emphasis)

Where we position ourselves within a field, and how we position others, is linked to the metafield of power, something which is undertheorized in Wenger's account. While his shift of focus away from the study of power as political and economic conflict towards power within 'social communities' (Wenger 1998, p. 189) enables us to understand organizations better, it is the interplay between the wider system and social life that is central to our concerns about practice. In particular, we do not just join a community without having an understanding of how our knowing is given distinction within wider structures of the economy and culture. Hence our knowing is related to the staking of claims to enter a field of practice and to be consecrated as knower. Hence in Wenger's language engagement, imagination and alignment are benign descriptors of what we do when we seek recognition through what Bourdieu describes as the staking symbolic capital:

All the manifestations of social recognition which make up symbolic capital, all the forms of perceived being which make up a social being that is known, 'visible', famous, admired, invited, loved, etc. are so many manifestations of the grace (*charisma*) which saves those it touches from the distress of an existence without justification ... there is no worse dispossession, no worse privation, perhaps, than that of the losers in the symbolic struggle for recognition, for access to a socially recognized social being, in a word, to humanity. This struggle is not reducible to a Goffmanian battle to present a favourable representation of oneself: it is competition for a power that can only be won from others competing for the same power, a power over others that derives its existence from others, from their perception and appreciation ... and therefore a power over a desire for power and over the object of this desire. (Bourdieu, 2000, p. 241)

Our entry into, and participation within, a community of practice is a dynamic power process because 'belonging to a group is something you build up, negotiate and bargain over, and play for' (Bourdieu 1990, p. 75) and Bourdieu's thinking tools of field and habitus enable us not only to understand practice but also to explain it. The emphasis is less on prescriptions as to how we ought to behave as company employees and more on how we are social and socializing agents through our practice.

Leading Teachers as social practice means that we can extend our gaze beyond securing teacher leadership towards the vibrancy of understanding meaning and experience, and how we struggle for change. Furthermore, it enables us to develop an understanding of distributed leadership within practice that recognizes and transcends the organizational boundaries. As social and socializing agents we can engage in the exercise of power as members of an organizational field but also positioning ourselves in regard to a wider metafield of power. Our positioning as Leading Teachers enables us to reveal our dispositions towards teaching and learning, and to generate our dispositions through such activity.

5 Developing Leading Teachers

Here are some questions to stimulate our thinking:

(a) Why can I be at the same place at different times, but not be at different places at the same time?

(b) Could scientists one day find out whether or not fish feel bored?

(c) Could there have been nothing?

(d) What are numbers?

(e) Is it rational to prefer a simple explanation of some phenomena to a more complex one?

(f) What is it for a sentence to be meaningless?

(g) Can it ever be true that it would have been better for someone if s/he had not been born?

(h) Is there anything which it is always wrong to do, however good the consequences of doing it?

(i) Are praise and blame relics of a pre-scientific attitude to people?

(j) When you try something and fail, how can you tell whether or not you could have succeeded?

(k) In deciding social policy, how much weight should be given to the interests of future generations?

(l) Is it ever justifiable to discriminate in favour of members of disadvantaged groups?

All of these questions have a place in the work of teachers. They are all questions that can be presented to students of a range of ages to enable dialogue, and we can imagine the creative thinking skills that could be developed and enhanced through access to and variations of such questions as (b) and the knowing that could be generated. They are all questions that are relevant to teachers in thinking about their work, and given the busyness of schools then (a) is probably lived everyday. However, have teachers experienced questions (d) or (f) in their training for the literacy and numeracy hours? In training on classroom management, are teachers asked to think about questions such as (g), (i) or (l)? In training for school leadership are teachers asked to think about questions such as (c), (e), (h), (j) or (k)?

These questions get to the core of the educational project: they ask respondents to think deeply in ways that are not easily resolvable. They are enduring questions that affect how we live our lives and how we make choices. Yet, the reaction could be one of negativity: these questions are esoteric and disconnected from the real world of work. This is particularly the case when I reveal that these are questions that Oxford entrants were asked to select from and write about on the afternoon of 24 November 1978. Four questions had to be chosen from a list of 30 split into two sections (general philosophy; moral and political philosophy) and answered in three hours (Colleges of Oxford University 1978). Hence a justifiable case could be made that these questions entertain and amuse academics over their long lunches, and through co-option into elite institutions sustain such practice, but do nothing to help practitioners in their engagement with Ofsted inspectors or in responding to a call from a concerned parent. Hence it is highly unlikely, and indeed unacceptable, for trainers to venture onto this territory, largely because the trainees would not accept it. The questions are IRRELEVANT. This chapter is about relevance: what it is and who controls what is and is not relevant knowing.

Capacity building

There is a marked shift in the literature focused on securing change from the school as a learning organization to capacity building:

> From a relatively simple perspective, capacity building is concerned with providing opportunities for people to work together in a new way. Collegial relations are therefore at the core of capacity building. One of the distinguishing features of schools that are failing is the sheer absence of any professional community, discourse and trust. Within improving schools, a climate of collaboration exists and there is collective commitment to work together. This climate is not simply given but is the deliberate result of discussion, development and dialogue among those working within the organization. An improving school community consists of teachers who are active in constructing meaning and collaborating in mutual enquiry and learning. An improving school is also a learning community where the learning of teachers receives the same attention as the learning of pupils. Relationships are therefore critically important in the school improvement endeavour. (Harris and Lambert 2003, p. 4)

> Capacity building creates intellectual capital by emphasizing the develop-
> ment of knowledge, competence, and skill of parents, teachers and other
> locals in the school community. As parents and other citizens are able
> to provide the support that students need to belong and to be successful
> at school, they get smarter, and smarter parents mean smarter students.
> Teacher development can help build the intellectual capital that teachers
> need to keep up by increasing their knowledge of the disciplines and the
> pedagogical-content knowledge teachers need to teach these disciplines
> effectively. (Sergiovanni 2001, p. 48)

While there has been a shift from the organization as learning to people
as learners there is still the same emphasis on integration. Capacity
building does not seem to acknowledge disadvantage and social injustice,
but instead of the organization being responsible for failing to learn it is
now the individual who is the focus of attention. Let us take the example
of Bob Hewitt who told the story of his resignation after 30 years in the
job as a drama teacher and more recently as subject leader (Hewitt and
Fitzsimons 2001, pp. 2–3)

Hewitt tells us that after the school was put into special measures
the new headteacher implemented an Ofsted recommendation that 'all
teachers were to write lesson plans broken down into five minute seg-
ments', and having refused to do this, a disciplinary hearing and an
appeal led to a final ultimatum to comply. He goes on to say:

> Lesson plans are as good a peg as any upon which to hang up my coat.
> Although the £2000 threshold would do just as well; or the health and
> safety rules that have banned my most challenging trust exercise even
> though I've used it for 20 years without accident; or the new reward system
> that are just cheap bribes; or the setting of targets that have nothing to do
> with educating children, and everything to do with performance related
> pay; or the management's fear of Ofsted; or the new culture of improving
> all schools by encouraging pupils to inform on their mates. To see schools
> these days as filled just with bureaucratic bullshit is to seriously miss the
> point, however. Education has traditionally been about freedom. But there
> is no freedom anymore. It's gone. Initiative and resourcefulness are banned.
> Every school has become a part of the gulag. How else would inspectors
> time the literacy hour with stopwatches, or a teacher be dismissed over a
> bit of missing paperwork? It's all right for me to say so, mind, I've no more
> mortgage to pay. The head and the governors want me to stay, and my
> colleagues urge me to stick with it. 'Just write the blooming lesson plans,
> Bob! The kids still need what you have to offer!' Well, maybe, but they'll
> get by. I'm not happy about leaving. I was hoping to find out whether I
> could still be cool at 65. And I don't know how to tell my pupils that I'm
> going. And if that father sends his kid to this school because he liked the

look of the drama teacher, I won't be there to teach him. But I value my sanity too much to stay. And one thing's for sure: they cannot run gulags on their own.

Is this capacity building? It could be argued that it is, because a teacher who is not ready to take the necessary risk to bring about a change in school needs to either obey or go. The teacher was unable to trust and be trusted, by arguing against the change the teacher was threatening social cohesion, and through dissent the required synergies for school improvement could not take place. Hence capacity building could be a form of professional cleansing where those who have knowledge and knowing that prevents the smooth and tidy improvement process to take place disappear. By acting in accordance with the instruction to write lesson plans in particular ways then teachers in the school are enabling oppression to take place, and so while the language of capacity building remains benign it is being experienced in a very malign way. Not least in the expectation that this work will happen without any additional time to do it. Consequently, teachers are incapacitated and respond accordingly, and the building that goes on is a fabrication of compliance with demands to structure teaching in ways that undermine agency.

Let's consider a different scenario. Research shows that social class remains a feature of educational attainment (Ball 2003b) and that students' participation in learning is affected by their pedagogic identity, which is structured through their socioeconomic context (Reay and Arnot 2004). The challenge lies in how we can enable differentiated student voices with positive and negative identities to join in capacity building for the school? Certainly, if the approach taken is one of accountability for control, as in Bob Hewitt's case, then as Fielding (2001) argues we will end up integrating students into structures rather than liberating them. Fielding gives an account of the 'Student as Researchers' project and how teacher–student research groups were formed and developed in ways that created democratic opportunities:

> As in Year 1, the impact of all three research groups was visible and significant. The most far reaching and most radical was the research and recommendations of the life skills group. In essence the students were saying three things. Firstly, they were puzzled as to why the school insisted that all tutors had to teach the life skills programme which included issues like adolescent sexuality and drug education. It was clear that a significant number of staff were embarrassed and thus ill-equipped to teach areas with particular sensitivities involved. Students felt embarrassed on their behalf and suggested greater involvement of external or highly motivated and trained people at particular points, including older students at the

school. Secondly, they highlighted an overdidactic, rather monochrome pedagogy that gave students little room to use IT skills or get involved in more active and engaging forms of learning. Lastly, and most radically, they challenged the whole model of curriculum that underpins current thinking and practice in the UK. What they were advocating was not a longer list of topics to choose from; rather they were arguing for a move away from curriculum as delivery to curriculum as the joint making of meaning. Whilst recognising the necessity of teacher perspectives and priorities informing the programme they nonetheless urged the school to acknowledge and incorporate their perspectives as students; a negotiated curriculum and a negotiated pedagogy seemed to them to make more sense as we approach the new century. The quality of the research and the elegance and strength of the students' advocacy, particularly at a substantial presentation to staff on a professional development day, has led to profound changes in the life skills curriculum. Even more remarkably and more radically, not only did the curriculum and its attendant pedagogies undergo significant change, the group monitoring and evaluating the impact of the new provision includes three students ... what we are witnessing here are profound cultural and structural changes in the professional identity and working practices of a large, very successful secondary comprehensive school, changes that are student-led and sustained by the richness and attentiveness of a dialogic culture. (pp. 127–8)

Fielding goes on to address the issues around how we build in emancipation rather than totality. Bob Hewitt had experienced totalizing through the sameness of teacher practice, and it is clear that pupils can experience this every day as they are shoe-horned into these externally prescribed lesson plan designs. If we are serious about building capacity then it does need to include students in ways other than seeking their views as clients of the curriculum, and as such Fielding argues for 'transversal politics' through which we learn about differences, and how to use dialogic encounters as 'radical collegiality' (p. 130) to engage with this. This approach to building capacity is highly political because it is about educational leadership, and it requires teachers to commit overtly to this values position. For this to happen teachers need to experience the type of freedom that Hewitt says we have lost, and have the security of knowing that in taking the risk of working with students in this way they will not be let down by being officially graded and labelled as failing. As Sergiovanni (2001) notes:

> Local capacity remains undeveloped, however, as long as the policy process itself – the ends of schooling, not just the means – is determined by the excessive use of mandates and incentives as the primary strategy for change and as the primary focus of leadership – a lesson not yet learned by leaders

who seek to enhance local autonomy while at the same time mandating
uniform standards and assessments. (p. 49)

Furthermore, as long as we keep the focus on school improvement
rather than improvement to teaching and learning then we will find
it difficult to enable educational leadership by teachers and students
to flourish. This is because the school as a unified organization to
be controlled in such a way as to deliver efficiently, effectively and
economically national targets and reform, is increasingly obsolete.
However, the school as an institution within a democratic system is
rather different, because an institution is about producing meaning and
contributes to wider cognitive and affective cultures. We need to question, support, reform, abolish and cherish our institutions and examine
the relationship with the state, but we cannot do that through an
institution just as an organization. The school as an institution of governance has to be understood in relation to the formal distribution and
exercise of power, and just because we have the internet, mobile phones
and chat-rooms we do not have to write off spaces for shared face-to-
face learning. All the democratic tendencies of the postwar period that
have been stifled by neoliberal restructuring from the New Right and
New Labour have the potential to re-emerge stronger than ever. This
is not just through the approaches outlined by Fielding, but due to the
types of changes that schools are being exhorted to embrace and take
risks with. For example, Blackmore (2000) shows that the school as
the centre of formal learning is being reconfigured around networks,
and the teacher as the 'authorizer of valued knowledge in schools' is
being reworked around

> ... their capacity to stimulate and tap into their students' needs and inter-
> ests through creative pedagogies that assist students to develop a capacity
> to distinguish and make judgements between data, information, knowledge
> and that encourage social values and behaviours which underpin a just
> and tolerant society. Teachers must become research practitioners, and
> systems must support teachers to develop reflexive professional capacities.
> (p. 385)

The consequence of this is that we have to address our approach to
knowledge and knowing, and how we enable teachers and students to
know and be knowledgeable.

Relevance

What is useful and useless knowledge and knowing, and who are the knowers that do or do not know, is crucial to how we proceed in developing educational leadership. When we stop for a moment to think about the complexities of teaching and learning, and the demands of organizational life, then the issue of relevance is put on to the agenda. Relevance could mean that you don't know the job of teaching if you don't do it, and as Ebbutt *et al.* (2000) show there are major cultural barriers between those who teach in schools and universities regarding the type and organization of work in different settings that could be obstacles to productive work. In a climate of fearfulness it then becomes axiomatic that teachers will declare the challenges to practice raised through research as irrelevant. Indeed, Hayes and Butterworth (2001) tell us that 'during 2000–2001, it is estimated that every school received three initiatives and 10 press releases each week!' (p. 358), and so what is and is not relevant can become buried in a morass of competing priorities and a sapping of energy.

Relevance could mean what is pertinent in the immediacy of the here and now, and so in the midst of teaching 35 eight-year-olds at 2 p.m. on a Friday afternoon it is highly unlikely that teachers will want to debate philosophical questions regarding numbers and sentences. Furthermore, given that workload extends beyond the working day into evenings and weekends, and so time on other interests and with family is compromised, then again it is highly unlikely that the purposes of schools and schooling will be on the agenda while juggling the ironing with the marking. When we combine this with the anti-intellectual approach to education and the demands on teachers in the last 20 years then it is not surprising that in the midst of exhaustion teachers might at best say: 'What has this got to do with …?' and at worst: 'Just tell me what to do and I will do it.' Impatience and frustration with intellectual work and compliance and resignation towards instrumental work should not be used to construct particular knowledge, knowing and knowers as either relevant or irrelevant. Such a binary is not helpful to those involved, and is a fabrication of how we do and should engage with and challenge day-to-day experiences in what is often labelled 'the real world'.

Relevance could be a way of justifying a particular approach to schools which needs research evidence to support it. Hence action research by teachers could be labelled as irrelevant because teachers are building on published research and constructing their own enquiry in ways that may not directly relate to the national policy agenda.

Indeed, Winch and Foreman-Peck (2000) argue that there are four main objections to teachers conducting their research: (1) lack of resources (time, money) means that research may not be useful; (2) case-study work does not have validity when dealing with large-scale issues; (3) teachers lack the research expertise to do effective research; and, (4) educational research is contaminated by ideological interests and rhetoric. They go on to argue that while research is integral to teacher practice, resources could be invested and skills developed, it is still the case that those outside the classroom – meaning outside schools and even education – may not be convinced regarding rigour. Nevertheless, they also show that relevance is a political issue, and that all the criticisms regarding teacher research can be dealt with (e.g. investment in research, larger-scale projects, training), and they argue that we do need to admit that centralized macro research agendas can be just as much contaminated by ideology as the microprojects of teachers in their classrooms.

Relevance could be constructed around what is of significance and importance for our work, and this could extend beyond the immediate to the wider purposes of schools and schooling. As I have argued so far, there is knowledge and ways of knowing that teachers should have access to and could have that access extended through professional development. Educational leadership as a social practice enables us to reflect upon our own epistemologies and the positions we take on knowledge creation. Those who are located in the natural sciences have a disposition towards positivistic and objective knowledge, and so experimentation and measurement are integral to how the truth is pursued. Those who are located in the humanities have a disposition towards meaning and how narratives can reveal the contested nature of our work and the subjectivity of connoisseurship when judging that work. Hence what is and is not relevant begins with our habitus as revealed through the knowledge and knowers that we position ourselves around. Attempts to structure and shape it through other knowledge claims are of interest here, and so teachers should have access to a range of knowing. They might reject it as irrelevant to them, but at least they have had the opportunity to do this, and they know where it is and how to access it if they or their circumstances change. On the other hand, access to this knowing might be a life-changing moment where new insights are developed. Teachers shouldn't have to experience negative epiphanies in the way that Bob Hewitt did, and neither should issues such as paying the mortgage mean that they have to comply with knowing that they reject and can feel is harmful to themselves and others. If teachers are going to build a sense of self for students and themselves then they will not only need training but also educational opportunities.

Developing teachers

Training is premised on certainty and is about determining certainty. What is to be known and how that knowing can be made visible is clear for those doing the training and for those who are to be trained. It could be that you are trained in a particular type of knowledge such as how to wire a plug or to make a cheese sauce. This requires the technical know how of which wires to attach to which part of the plug or how to make a roux prior to adding the milk, and could include how to hold a screwdriver or how to switch on a cooker. Training can be more than the technical and might venture into deeper levels of knowledge regarding what is going on in a plug or in a saucepan that will enable you to understand better what happens when a plug is used or when a pan is heated. Furthermore, the affective side of skills can be developed regarding how you feel about the work, and so the importance of what you do and the sense of achievement is developed. The apprenticeship system (mentoring and coaching) can be used to enable the transference of craft knowledge, where hints and tips that have always worked are passed on to the learner, and within this a sense of pride and satisfaction with a job well done can be imbued.

Training teachers in pre or inservice is challenging for us. If we wanted to train teachers in teaching then we would have to have some certainty regarding what teaching is and how it should be done. However, teaching is not a function such as wiring or a chemical reaction such as cooking but is a human relationship. To train teachers we would have to approach aspiring and serving teachers as trainable based on identified needs. We have to operate as if the knowledge was settled and use ways of communicating that knowledge so that it would be accepted. Because teaching is about human relationships then we need to control the uncontrollable through knowing how to use the voice, the body and presence, in combination with knowing how to question and how to organize learning groups. But we also need to know how to use judgement in making decisions in the midst of complexity, and because we cannot control everything then we need to be able to respond to the unpredictable. We should then be in a position to witness teaching in operation in the classroom, and we would be able to break down what is said and done in ways that allow the features of good practice to be identified, and then put back together again in the form of a grade. Training assumes assessment where the trainee and at least one other can observe and measure conformance with what is required. Some will grasp what is needed immediately, while others will work through a trial-and-error approach in order to achieve the required standard.

Currently, the body of knowledge that is officially required of aspiring and serving teachers is laid out by the Teacher Training Agency [TTA], (2003) in three main sections (professional values and practice; knowledge and understanding; teaching) with a total of 42 descriptive statements regarding practice. Approaching the preparation and development of teachers in this way has its advantages. There is a clear set of standards that all have to meet, and the procedures set up to deliver are controlled through contract compliance and external inspection. Training means that we can distinguish between a particular type of knowing, such as how to question a student, from everyday interactions such as holding a conversation with a student. Furthermore, a person can be licensed and their conduct controlled by themselves and by the community in which they have been accepted. However, a long-term career based only on training is a rather sterile and instrumental approach to what is a potentially rich and exciting relationship between all members of the school community. It positions the teacher as automatically and enduringly in a deficit situation with needs, and it presents what is to be known and practised as 'musts' regarding what is known and is worth knowing. These training imperatives are communicated in instrumental texts and bullet-points, and so knowledge is controlled into bite-sized chunks that can be easily digested. Such an approach is consistent with electronic computerized database and presentation systems, and so knowledge can be accessed and articulated through unambiguous statements of practice. This approach to knowledge denies the person who is the trainer and the trained, and the trainer is meant to be the neutral conduit through which knowledge is passed and the trained is the neutral recipient of such knowledge. The trainer is given a script of required props (officially sanctioned texts) and activities (officially sanctioned control processes) and the trainee is expected to cooperate. Such over reliance on simplified know how is fast becoming the embalming fluid of education: you can be made to look good but you are in effect brain dead (Gunter and Willmott 2002). The process is one of conformity and compliance, and yet the knowledge and know how is fundamentally ideological and political.

As teaching is a power to and power over relationship, then it is based on assumptions about the position of the teacher and the learner, and if we reposition the student as knower then we can give primacy to the processes of knowing around understanding the purposes of knowing.

In particular, as Watkins and Mortimore (1999) show, the shift towards learners as thinkers and capable of metacognition means that the potential exists for them not only to know something but to understand the situation in which they have learned and used it. Once we know about knowing in context then we can know how and why contexts are different, and so how our learning can and cannot be used within those contexts.

Who are regarded as the knowers in this relationship and how that knowing is developed remains a feature of how we might proceed. Two examples illustrate. Winkley (1998) in talking about the preparation of heads notes that training can happen at any time, as and when, but it is the philosophical questions of meaning that need to be developed for headship. Leitch and Day (2001) report on how educationalists from a range of educational institutions were engaged with an EdD module on reflective practice, and how the challenge of their work showed the need for professional learning to make explicit issues regarding self-esteem and self-worth. Both examples tell us that we need a different approach to knowing as smooth and tidy ring-binder processes that secure officially approved outcomes. Not least because if we relate these points to teachers and students then we can see that they need to be able to develop a sense of purpose and to understand what underpins their work, and this requires both the teacher and the student to have access to thinking through what they are doing and why they are doing it.

Teachers need space to do such work. It should not be hurried into a twilight session or a precious weekend. Certainly teachers will want to support their work through investing their own resources in their learning, and teaching is a way of life because we cannot rationally and fully separate work and life. Dean (2001) suggests that the time is right for the government to 'revive the concept of the sabbatical' because, as he argues, 'mid-career refreshers are surely to be preferred to mid-career drop-out' and could enable teachers to be able to challenge the situation that many have complied with (p. 497). In this setting developing teachers through a critical evaluation of knowing and knowledge allows us to ask questions about: (1) the means by which knowledge has been generated, and so we would be interested in the techniques of how we know and how valid or reliable the knowing is; (2) who are regarded as the knowers and why, and so we would be interested in who has done the work and who has declared the knowing as valid and reliable; and (3) the institutions that support and sustain knowers and knowing over time, and so we would be interested in the promotion and consecration of knowers and knowing. In this way, teachers and students are able to ask about 'the prevailing order of the world' (Cox 1981, p. 129), and so you not only learn how to problem solve but also to problem pose, and to ask where what is problematic is generated from, by whom and for what purpose. The internet is a wonderful resource, but it is also full of rubbish – and some dangerous rubbish – and we can only use it as knowledge if we know how to engage critically with it. Hence education means that you are not just trained to do but can also know why you are trained and how you can control the use of that training. By having training needs you can ask about who is determining those needs and what the claims are for legitimacy. You not only have needs but you also have interests in how your work is located within the wider scheme of learners and learning, and so your orientation is not just to enable the school as an organization to be successful but to the wider goals of the democratic development of the institutions we have inherited or created. Teaching is ideological and political, and we need to recognize that our commitment to democratic development of self and the student as self, and the interplay within the collective, is vital. If we do not have a belief in democratic processes and the creation of opportunities to develop democratic dispositions then our place within a school as an institution of democracy is not secure.

Knowers and knowing

Conceptually informed practice cannot just be trained. Yes, we can learn the techniques of research design and analysis, but developing a life-long commitment to understanding our own and others' knowledge claims requires access to knowledge and knowing that training alone cannot deliver. If we begin with the teacher and the student as knowers and how we develop conceptually informed practice through how they use and produce what is known and is worth knowing then we immediately hit the enduring issue of the link between knowledge and democracy. Historically, the two have been seen as incompatible as knowledge has been controlled by elites (Church, state, universities, corporations) and access to it has been limited, and even the advent of mass education in the postwar period was still based on learning technologies (lecture, seminar, reading, essay writing) that officially consecrate particular types of knowledge creation opportunities.

As Delanty (2001) argues, the challenge for us in educational institutions is the democratization of knowledge, and an important starting point for educational leadership is the difference between data, information and knowledge. Schools are meant to be data-rich environments from the teacher mark book through to attendance statistics, combined with externally calculated numbers in the form of league tables. Data are not information or knowledge. Information is created when we use data for a particular purpose such as a threshold application form or an Ofsted report, while knowledge 'is related to the cognitive structure of society'. Delanty (2001) goes on to argue that

> I do not see knowledge only as a matter of expertise. By knowledge I mean the capacity of a society for learning, a cognitive capacity that is related to the production of cultural models and institutional innovation. In the contemporary context, the penetration of knowledge into all spheres of life is clearly one of the major characteristics of the age. We are living in a knowledge society in the sense that social actors have even greater capacities for self-interpretation and action. Professional knowledge and lay knowledge are less separate than they used to be. The idea of the knowledge society refers also to something more basic: the opening up of new cognitive fields which have a reflexive relation to knowledge. (p. 5)

Consequently, the school as an institution of the state has traditionally been a place where officially developed knowledge (through the Church, university and corporations) regarding the mind and body has been used by teachers to produce social agents. This has, over time, been used either to deliberately create, or is a consequence of, a differentiated society in regard to who has access to particular types of knowledge and how this structures life opportunities.

The knowledge society means that knowledge producers are growing in number, and the school as a user of a wide range of knowledge and as a place of knowledge production is developing rapidly. But we should not confuse wider access to knowledge with democracy, and we need to reveal the enduring link with the state. In discussing the place of the university in this knowledge society Delanty (2001) argues that: 'the disciplinary structure of knowledge and the nation state no longer totally define the cognitive field of knowledge' (p. 6) and so what counts as knowledge and knowing is becoming multidisciplinary and even though the state subsidizes education it is struggling to control what should be known and is worth knowing. In that sense the state has shifted from 'a provider state' to that of a 'a regulatory agency' (p. 8), and so it is seeking to form new relationships with the individual who uses the internet through to the large corporation which can move work around the globe. In compulsory education the state still retains its role as the main provider, but it is the case that incremental privatization based on the bidding culture for resources combined with the audit culture for standards means that schools increasingly face regulation. This has been increased through the creation of quangos (TTA [Teacher Training Agency], Ofsted, NCSL) and as agents of the state they do the regulation through the prescription, training and measurement of good practice. Indeed, proposition 10 from the think-tank at the NCSL states that school leadership needs a 'champion' who will lead the debate 'in the country, with teachers, senior managers, governors, communities educational officers and politicians'. As the 'champion' the NCSL is 'an agency sufficiently powerful to make the argument, to develop and implement programmes in partnership and to link together policies and other agencies' (Hopkins 2001, pp. 14–15). It is through this regulation that the interlinking of the structure of knowledge and the nation-state is being reworked and strengthened.

Other knowledge users and producers such as LEAs (local education authorities) and universities are being brought under the same regulatory regime, and so the spaces to contest official knowledge and knowers are being squeezed, and indeed we can witness how in the last decade or so these institutions have been caricatured as increasingly irrelevant. Hence the drive towards the democratization of knowledge within our field, that has been a feature from its earliest days, is in danger of being lost. The approach taken by field members in higher education from the 1960s begins with describing practice and seeking to understand practice. The argument was that by giving practitioners access to a pluralism of knowledge, from their own theorizing and the social sciences, then they can engage with their practice in new and interesting ways. While we may read about problems in the preparation of leaders within higher education this tends to be focused on the USA, where the Theory Movement meant that knowledge was determined by the professors, and we should not assume the direct applicability of these criticisms to England. Indeed, research demonstrates that those who brought the field into the teaching and research curriculum of the university came themselves from a school and/or LEA, and so we should regard these field members as having relocated their practice within an education system rather than being outside of the so-called real world of schools (Gunter 1999).

The dynamism of the field through pluralistic provision of postgraduate work and more recently professional doctorates, has enabled practitioners to have a choice of where they wanted to study, and the opportunity for short- and long-term development. They could access study at different stages in their personal and professional lives, and use the study to develop informal networks of mentors and friends that could endure. What has limited their engagement has been a lack of resources: teachers often pay for their own professional development and study in their own time.

Enabling teachers to develop as users and producers of knowledge, and to be knowledgeable through critical evaluation when in receipt of other types of knowledge, means that the evidence base on which policy decisions are made are open to scrutiny. Masters and doctoral work is not about delivering national standards but is about challenging and often exceeding those standards. The teacher is able to engage productively with a text and arguments in ways that not only seek to understand but can develop as well. In this way teachers are not oppositional but are policy-makers too, and through conceptually informed practice they can use their judgement to respond to tips for teachers as well as wider questions of student attainment and learning.

Through intellectual work teachers are also public intellectuals: they can speak with and on behalf of themselves and others, and so challenge what Smith (1997, p. 1) calls the 'tyranny of tidiness'. This requires a rethinking of how we understand professional practice, and it is less about conforming to an abstract professionalism or elite status and more about what Sachs (2000, p. 77) describes as 'the activist professional'. Activism is based on collegiality and on research which is necessarily political, and so teachers cannot only understand what they are doing but the context in which they are doing it. Jones (2004, p. 22) argues that such activism is not just about rebuilding trust with the public but is more about 'an education counter-politics' where teachers engage in shaping policy through popular movements that can lead reform and resist damaging reforms.

Teachers already do their work in public and have a strong affiliation to the classroom, but they don't have to be in it all of the time to be close to practice. Indeed, they can be close and distant to their practice while teaching as they engage in activity and do actions, but they can also be close to practice in a seminar room with other educationalists as activity and actions can be problematized and provided for. Educationalists from all parts of the education system experience similar types of delights and pressures, and sharing this and seeking to understand it enables the field to be a vibrant place. In doing this we are not letting the children down or avoiding our responsibilities: 'We need public intellectuals, but for intellectual debate to thrive we also need our own independent space. Not an ivory tower to hide in, but institutions that are not ashamed of the idea that sometimes it is worthwhile developing ideas because it is exciting' (Furedi 2001, p. 17).

As the story of Bob Hewitt illustrates, teaching is being made teacher-proof, and this suits the elites who control schools and the headteachers who put the technical implementation of reform before educational purposes. It is also very easy to construct dissent as sedition, and it is understandable that teachers are reluctant to stand up and be counted. A diet of training will only secure a safe position and so the potential to generate ideas, so essential to democratic development, could be lost.

If field members are only allowed to be legitimate knowers through contract provision with the government and its agencies, then what place does the field member have in addition to that of doing entrepreneurial work? Delanty (2001) makes some important observations regarding the university in general, and in ways that challenge assumptions about a hierarchy of knowledge:

> ... I would like to clarify the question of what kind of knowledge is produced by the postmodern university in the age of technological and cultural citizenship. There are four kinds of knowledge, to which correspond four knowledge producers. The university fosters the following kinds of knowledge: (1) research, (2) education, (3) professional training, and (4) intellectual inquiry and critique. The first pertains to basic research and the accumulation of information. The second relates to human experience and the formation of personality. The third concerns the practical task of vocational training and accreditation for professional life, while the fourth deals with the wider public issues of society and relates to the intellectualization of society. Corresponding to each of these are the roles of the expert, the teacher, the professional trainer and the intellectual. With respect to citizenship, the domains of education and intellectual inquiry and critique relate to cultural citizenship, and the domains of research and professional training relate to technological citizenship. The fulfilment of these two kinds of citizenship is the social responsibility of the university. To find ways of linking these roles and cognitive frameworks into a communicative understanding of the university seems to be what the university needs to achieve today if it is to be able to take on the task of becoming one of the key institutions in the public sphere and in which citizenship is brought forward on to new levels. (pp. 8–9)

The university remains a place where teachers can access all four types of knowledge and so the potential exists to develop the school as a place for the further development of this knowledge. It is curious that the accreditation of leaders has been given to agencies of the government, particularly since the field in higher education has worked hard not to lay claim to having a monopoly of knowledge. For example, partnerships with LEAs have been fundamental to course design and development from the 1960s, and this diversity has enabled practitioners to be seen as something more substantial than users of research (Gunter 1999).

The challenge for government has been that the university is not a unified sector, has its own systems of quality assurance and has procedures for scrutinizing the knowledge claims of professional bodies. Furthermore, the commitment to research, education and intellectual enquiry means that pluralism in knowledge production and a commitment to conceptually informed practice is likely not to produce compliant and fearful teachers. The tradition of the public intellectual is stronger here, and as such we don't easily herd into teams but are concerned to challenge the team about what they are doing and why. The opportunity exists for field renewal and development within the university, and as I am arguing, we will not leave the field quietly. Much does depend on how we respond to the misinformation about who we are and what we do, and we do need robust educational leadership in the higher education sector as well. Nevertheless, the field in higher education can continue to work in Delanty's (2001) terms for a university in the public sphere as 'the most important site of interconnectivity' (p. 6) so that we can participate in and shape field discourses. We can do this through knowledge production, and we can generate ideas that suggest alternatives to those being officially consecrated. If we want teachers to be public intellectuals then we in higher education have to grasp this opportunity as well. Our ideas are not commodities to be bought and sold, but are central to how we want to work and live together, and as such our disenfranchisement from education is also in our own hands.

How might we do this? In an age of media constructed celebrity it is difficult for the field to chart a way forward. In staking symbolic capital we need to distinguish between the rigour of research within professional practice from the pundits who can promote but who do not necessarily generate ideas (Bourdieu 2000). The demands of the bidding and audit culture in higher education have created the same work intensification and fears affecting lives and relationships as those experienced by teachers in schools and further education. Our strength in the field of educational leadership is in research and professional development underpinning by our practitioner-academic habitus (Gunter 2001). We do know about teaching and learning because we have done it and continue to do it, and the pressures that teachers have are ones that we face as well. We are inspected and graded. We know about leading and managing because we do it. Who we are and how we do our work needs to be more clearly articulated, not least by more research papers about higher education that teachers should read. Hughes (1985) is famed for having articulated heads as leading professionals and chief executives, but what is not often talked about is how he did this through comparing his data and ideas on heads with leaders in other parts of the education system. These days we would be hard pressed to find papers on school leadership that used knowledge and knowing from further and higher education to illuminate and develop what goes on in schools. We have to fight such narrowness through our scholarship, and we have to orientate ourselves towards our position within knowledge production.

Successive governments have taken a huge risk in turning their backs on educational intellectuals, and yet we need to remain optimistic because such work continues to take place and to live in practice. In a recent ESRC-funded seminar series Challenging the Orthodoxy of School Leadership, knowledge workers from a range of educational sites in the UK, Australia, New Zealand, Canada and the USA, came together in four seminars to examine the current state of the field and to generate new perspectives on how we might work for change. At the Birmingham seminar (Gunter 2003b) ten practitioners from schools, colleges and LEAs talked about practice and research, and gave their reflections about the meaning this had for educational leadership. In leading the talk about leadership the ten practitioners were able to experience Winter's (1991) conceptualization of the stories about their working lives: (1) using theories as the means of enabling experience to be interpreted and reinter-preted; (2) engaging in dialectics as the process of rigorous reflection on and within experience; (3) working together in seminar groups to devel-oping knowing; (4) enabling voices to be heard through developmental writing and through publishing ideas. Such an approach enabled the long-established partnership between educational leaders across a range of institutions to meet within a university setting that has remit to give permission to knowledgeable people to talk about their experiences in ways that are not to be moulded into reform compliance or consecrated as preferred knowledge (Gunter *et al.* 2003).

6   Leading Leading Teachers

Work, work, work

Sociological work is implicated in the very world that it seeks to describe and understand. In doing this work we have to recognize the strength of our contribution rather than apologize for it. This book is essentially insider scholarship: I am a teacher and I will remain a teacher, and through research I can enable teachers and teaching. Bauman (2000) encapsulates this perfectly:

> There is no choice between 'engaged' and 'neutral' ways of doing soci-
> ology. A non-committal sociology is an impossibility. Seeking a morally
> neutral stance among the many brands of sociology practised today, brands
> stretching all the way from the outspokenly libertarian to the staunchly
> communitarian, would be a vain effort. Sociologists may deny or forget the
> 'world-view' effects of their work, and the impact of that view on human
> singular or joint actions, only at the expense of forfeiting that responsibility
> of choice which every other human being faces daily. The job of sociology
> is to see to it that the choices are genuinely free, and that they remain so,
> increasingly so, for the duration of humanity. (p. 216)

Hence reading this text is not about consecrating a canon or the burning of a book, it is a chart of the field that should be engaged with in ways that generate perspective and new insights. This book is about knowledge production and is itself a part of the process of knowledge production. In presenting this reading of education then an account is written, and so the past, present and future can be worked for in ways that enliven rather than embalm, disrupt rather than sedate.

The position I take, and one that is non-negotiable, is that teachers cannot go on experiencing quantitative and qualitative overload in their work, or working to make this impossible situation work better. It is destroying their humanity, largely because as Ozga (2000b) argues meaning has been stripped out of their working lives, and modernization is resulting in teachers being 'disconnected from their fundamentally important role in building citizenship' (p. 356). Students could draw the conclusions from this that teachers' work is neither doable nor valuable.

Crucially, it is work that they themselves may not aspire to do. They will lack respect for an occupational group that has been identified as the prime cause of their failure to thrive in education. Furthermore, students learn that in a world of 'insecurity', 'uncertainty' and 'unsafety' (Bauman 2000, p. 161) encounters such as teaching and learning in the classroom can only be about 'instant gratification' (p. 162) and so are consumable and disposable. However, forging human relations need not be this risky; indeed it shapes who we are and could become, and teachers have a central role in enabling this within the space and time of educational experiences. For authentic agency to be advocated then it has to begin with the realities of practice rather than the exhortation of so-called good practice, and in this sense I am beginning this final chapter with a sense of optimism. Helsby (1999) reassures us:

> ... it remains to be seen what educational policies will emerge and how the system of schooling will be changed in the future. The only thing that can be said with any certainty is that teachers themselves will continue to play a key role in any developments, since teaching can never be regulated and supervised by labour on a production line. Accordingly, the future nature of teachers' work will be shaped not only by imposed structures but also by the accumulation of choices made by individual teachers working in a variety of cultures and contexts. It is this balance of power and influence which provides a safeguard against the dangers of domination of schooling by fashionable dogmas or autocratic prescription and which gives hope for the future education of young people. (p. 175)

A construction of the future through educational leadership as a social practice is based on our understanding of the self and others, as individuals and within communities, as knowledge producers within a production that is structured and can be structured.

Educational leadership: one field or many?

Educational leadership is one field, but with a range of positions within it. School leadership is one of those positions: it is emerging, it is structurally privileged, and as such it is strong and potentially hegemonic. In contrast, knowledge production within educational leadership is (1) *multisite* within the home, the street, the school, the university, town hall and Whitehall; (2) *multilevel* within the teaching and learning process, it is inclusive of students and begins with them and those who work with them; (3) *multiprocess* by knowing through doing, through reflection on that doing, through data gathered about that doing and through theorizing about that data and the doing; (4) *multi-knowledge* by drawing on a range of social science theories that can be used to describe and explain practice. Educational leadership as knowledge production is advantageous for us because it means that we are able to chart the knowers, knowing and knowledge as it was, is, and might be, and so we can give recognition to the power dimensions.

It can be the case that those who know may not be regarded as being in the know because knowers are enabled or marginalized through the staking of cultural and symbolic capital (Bourdieu 2000). Similarly, there are those who claim to know, and are celebrated for this, but they only represent a particular position within the field. Certain types of knowers are being consecrated and we need to recognize the rise of the knowledge entrepreneur who buys and sells know how within a marketplace (Thrupp and Willmott 2003). Other types of knowers such as teachers are being marginalized as not knowing the game that needs to be played and so are having their work structured for them. Knowledge is increasingly determined by those at a distance from where knowing is to take place, and this knowing is translated into policy and training packages. Other knowing is not to be known, and the university as a site of contested knowing is increasingly suspect because purposes are about developing knowledge and knowing through research and critical dialogue. Access to pluralistic knowledge from within the social sciences enables the field member (student, teacher, parent, headteacher, councillor) to know about knowledge claims and hence listen to and engage with a range of voices about educational issues. We will struggle productively over educational goals and processes, and there will be difficulties, but these are the bread and butter of social and socializing encounters that cannot be easily silenced. Teachers need to know about knowledge and knowing if they are to know about teaching and learning as central to the human condition. To deny this access through a relentless diet of technical training is to deny both the realities and potentialities of the job.

Educational leadership is based on three main arguments. First, Leading Teachers conceptualized as effective teacher leadership is a very narrow and potentially conformist model of practice. We need to acknowledge and develop access to Leading Teachers as located within opportunities to develop meaning and to explore experiences, combined with becoming politically active through working for change. These areas of knowledge and knowing with their integral knowers provide teachers with a richer and deeper understanding of themselves and their sense of purpose. If we want to improve student experiences and outcomes as a result of a dozen or so years of formal education then we at least have to enable teachers to have access to knowing and knowledge in its widest sense. We cannot expect teachers who face a distant didactic pedagogy within external policy implementation to then question this approach in their own practice with students.

A second argument is that we need to understand the context in which teachers and their work are located. Schools are self-managing business organizations within the quasi-market, and so teachers' work has been restructured to deliver outcomes to students, parents and communities as consumers. This model is based on a restricted view of education as being a privilege of an economic elite and a rejection of the school as a public institution within an education system. In the postwar period the connection of the individual school to other schools through a commitment to the public good and to the wider community was strengthened. However, this struggle for an education system that is inclusive for all, and that not only widened participation but also created democratic opportunities through that inclusion, is one where progress has been cut short. The New Right in the 1970s and 1980s worked to condemn democratic development, and so as Ranson (2003) shows accountability is now narrowly hierarchical through being 'held to account', and so we face a 'summons to compliance' rather than an invitation to build trust:

> ... this discursive practice of accountability is not merely confined to organizational procedure, but defines the reasonableness of communication that must inform any just civil society. The obligations we have to each other; that is, to give and take reasons/accounts for our beliefs and actions, enable mutual understanding and agreement. Accountability in this view, as discursive reason, is the very expression rather than denial of our reflective agency. Our accounts of action make intelligible their intentions and the narrative histories we have authored and are responsible for. (pp. 460–61)

Repositioning around community ideals has retained the emphasis on creating unity, not primarily through the organization but through beliefs. While this has given heart to those who feel stifled by systems and demoralized by markets, there is a danger that we are seeking to live and work in a community as a theme park rather than community as diverse and dialogic. We cannot build workable communities that eschew politics, and so we need to engage with how we build productive political practice within and between networks. The potential exists for a better understanding of the interplay between networks and communities. Networks show teachers as being in the midst of political activity, and work in ways that both enable and frustrate. We cannot cleanse away the biographies of those who are teachers. We cannot train away strategy, negotiation and the exercise of power. We cannot completely manage away bad behaviour or insanity, as both exist, and no doubt will continue to do so, in our organizations, no matter how much we would prefer that they didn't. However, if we regard a school as a site within the field of educational leadership through which the habitus of those for whom the school serves is revealed within practice then we can begin to see community as an arena of struggle and dialogue over purposes, and we can understand the dispositions of those who are positioning and being positioned in particular ways.

A third argument builds on the other two. The first argument is concerned to acknowledge agency in a wider sense than delivering change, and the second argument is concerned to acknowledge structure in a more realistic sense than unification, and so the third argument is about how we understand the interlinking of this agency with structure. If agency is about access to a wider knowing, and if structure is about positioning that knowing within a field of social practice, then the interplay between the two is located in knowledge production as research. If we want to work for a more authentic capacity building then conceptually informed practice means that teachers are able to control their decision making and choices based on a range of resources such as their experience, habits, reading, training and evidence. Teachers need to know about how and why knowledge is produced and used, and how they are directly located within it. The ringbinders they are issued with are a power structure with particular knowledge claims, and the people who produce them and the trainers who are meant to deliver them are not neutral conduits through which knowledge flows.

The consequences of these arguments are that we have to have a more mature and realistic understanding of our context and of the people (warts and all) who inhabit that context. Excluding talented and committed people through retirement packages, low wages or other means is just not acceptable. We also have to ask more sensible and deeper questions than those being asked about school improvement and effectiveness. If we want improved and more effective teaching and learning then we need to focus on the relationship between teacher and student within contexts, because it is only through understanding interactions that we will be able to confront what we are concerned about and work for what we want to achieve. There are two consequences to this: first, how we position the student; and second, how we position formal leaders. In doing this I would want to acknowledge that in focusing on the teacher in this book I have created the opportunity for myself and others to take the issues of students and role incumbents forward in more depth in other projects, but in the space I have available I would like to contribute to creating the agenda for dialogue.

The arguments surrounding educational leadership point inevitably to the conclusion that students' learning and their well-being within and through that learning is core to field purposes. If we extend the arguments I have made in support of the development of teachers to that of students then we can engage in a much more considered dialogue about teaching and learning. Teachers who understand the school within a field and who recognize their own dispositions and those of others will be better placed to enable students to develop a sense of identity. Teachers who can own their work and have a justifiable model of their practice so that they know what they are doing and, more importantly, why they are doing it, can also work with students to enable this to be developed for them. Students who are in the know about this can also help teachers in their learning journey as well. This builds on the case that has already been made that learning is active, and we meet and greet this learning afresh everyday through our social and socializing encounters with each other. Formal learning through schools builds on and develops this construction, and so rejects the school as a warehouse to store students that the law demands must be educated and embraces the school as an active site of development:

> If we make the student the worker, then ... schooling has to change. The student now enters more actively into the learning process. Learning is the active engagement of the student, including all the sensitivities, points of view, talents, and imagination that he or she possesses, with the material under study, whether it is a short story, an algebraic operation, a question in biology, a comparison of the technique of Matisse with that of Pissarro, or his or her own poem about the season of spring. In the process of learning, and as a result of their active engagement with the material, students are asked to produce something that expresses their learning. (Starratt 2003, p. 160)

Those in formal role positions in schools, such as headteachers, senior managers and middle managers, only matter because they are teachers and do not matter more than teachers or students. Let me say more about this.

Much of what is written about securing change in education is based on teacher leadership which because of its underlying epistemology is automatically linked to role incumbents as organizational leaders. If teachers are to be formal and/or informal leaders within the organization then this role and the associated work is dependent on those who are organizationally superior to them. Hence we read about the paradox that teacher leadership depends on headteachers enabling it to happen (Jackson 2003) or that teacher leadership depends on the transformational behaviours and attributes on heads (Leithwood 2003). We need to look at the world differently. Headteachers, senior managers and middle managers are all teachers, and they should begin the week and the day on this basis. They have to work with students inside and outside the classroom as their prime purpose. If they do not have teaching and learning responsibilities then they should not be working in a school. Headteachers who do not teach are not acceptable and are not credible to students, to teachers or to the wider community. Hence those with formal organizational roles are legitimate first and foremost through their credentials as teachers and in their practice in teaching. In this way all that I have argued applies to them, and they are positioned within educational leadership and they should be participants in this leadership.

In the emergence of school leadership it has been the case that the organization has mattered more than the people who are meant to deliver its goals. Hence the headteacher's traditional role in the hierarchy, which is a product of our class and gendered society (Grace 1995), has been strengthened and developed through restructuring. In order to enable the policies of the New Right, and more recently New Labour, to be implemented then headteachers have been made central to educational restructuring, but while the rhetoric has been benign through the emphasis on building a vision and mission they have in reality been positioned as middle managers (Gunter 2001). Consequently, the organizational role of the headteacher in securing and keeping control, and in making the approved cultural changes to school workforce language and behaviour, has been emphasized and enabled through state-licensed training. The official job of role incumbents has been to deliver national targets so that political goals are achieved through the disciplinary structures of surveillance and performativity.

Research shows that there is dissent and some resistance, and headteachers (and their colleagues) have not been easily bought off. However, organizational matters are not necessarily the reasons why this is so, and in the end it is the commitment of role incumbents as teachers with other teachers that has enabled the professional courage to do what makes sense for students and the school workforce rather than automatically accepting non-educational structuring processes (Gunter 2001). If we reorientated ourselves within educational leadership then we would not automatically credit role incumbents with the gift of insight into strategic and long-term issues, and neither would we retreat into our classrooms and say: 'That it is nothing to do with me', or 'You're paid to do that.' Instead, if the classroom teacher and the headteacher both experienced professional development together then both would put teaching and learning at the core of their activity, and would necessarily accept the difference in emphasis on how they view their work in relation to organizational development. Headteachers outside the classroom only matter more to the extent that they currently do because of a combination of historical and policy prescriptions. We had the opportunity in the postwar period to engage with history differently, and so create other approaches to how we might want to structure our schools. As noted above, research evidence shows that heads do go against the grain and do work with their colleagues in a radical and collegiate way. This is not easy. It is permanently under threat and needs to be worked for by teachers and their students every day. We cannot necessarily change the world overnight, and there will be matters on which we might, for the moment, be prepared to make concessions. However, educational leadership requires us to recognize and practise the exercise of power in ways that are productive and enable our role in knowledge production to be as visible as possible.

The self and others

We cannot romanticize the consequences of educational leadership for students, or for teachers as teachers and as role incumbents. We have to live and work within structures that continue to shape and structure our agency in ways that are non-educational. We inherit ways of doing things and are directed to do things that challenge how we want to do it and expect to do it. While compromise is a valuable and necessary strategy if we are to survive, in the longer view, however, we need to think in terms of more than just survival if we want to enable students to be vibrant learners. If we want authentic development then we also need to establish the ways in which we want to work. Bates (2003) has helped our thinking on this through developing perspectives in answer to the question: can we live together? He argues that this question needs to be pursued through focusing on two main issues: (1) ethics, or 'how we are to respect each other's differences'; and (2) arrangements, or 'how we can construct and operate institutions that will allow us to work together cooperatively to redress current inequities and advance a common good while respecting each others' differences' (p. 2). Not only are these tough questions, but they are being asked of people who have learned that they are not worthy to be included in asking them, never mind discussing them. The attack on systems and the unleashing of markets, combined with the disregard for meaning and experience has generated a 'low trust' culture (Bates 2003, p. 7). We are asking people to take a risk at a time when they have had the confidence knocked out of them, and asking them to commit to something that they have no guarantee of being a part of. Starratt (2003, pp. 52–3) states: 'Now that we have some sense of the shift away from naïve optimism to awareness of the struggle, where do we as educators go from here? How do we attend to the task of administering meaning in a world so uncertain about which meanings to embrace?' Central to the argument here is that the development of school leadership is based on teachers not being trusted with the education of the nation's children, and as such they have positioned themselves accordingly. If we are to renew that trust then we need to enable teachers to develop their identities and practices through knowledge, knowing and access to a range of knowers, and I acknowledge that the challenge is how we do this when teachers have been told, and repeatedly told (often through censorship), that this does not matter to them. Hence trust has to be rebuilt across the education system, and indeed the public sector as a whole. If we don't want LEAs or universities to have a role in education then we should at least debate it rather than kill it off by stealth or neglect.

This trust does not have to be by an agreement to all believe the same thing, or to be from the same ethnic group, or to worship in the same way, or to have the same sexual orientation, or to be of the same gender. Central to practising our own complex identities is that we need to respect, bond with and recognize those who are different to us. As Bates (2003) states we don't all have to be converted or be dominated or cleansed, but we do need to live together in ways that respect differences, and we need public institutions that will allow our differences to be respected and worked through, and so 'all ways of life are continuously held up to scrutiny and evaluation' (p. 13). Furthermore, it does not mean that numeracy or literacy cannot be taught, but what it does mean is that established ways of knowing can be understood as constructions rather than immutable truths. Resisting conformity is our greatest challenge:

> The moral basis of the school as an institution must, then, be a defence of the individual rights of all pupils to freedom and equality, and to cultural, political and economic rights to the development of those capabilities through which they can create their selves and contribute to the wider society. This moral basis cannot be established in any school that practises exclusion, nor in any school that fails to provide the basis for communication between individuals pursuing diverse and defensible ways of life. The role of the school then is to protect the individual rights of all pupils and provide for communicative action between the differing ways of life that they value or could come to value, within the context of the school. This implies that the instrumental processes of the school need to be matched

with normative processes. These are unlikely to be achieved through current conceptions of the school as a performative agency related princi-pally to the interests of economic organizations. They are more likely to be achieved by schools which build into their practices activities that help form the capacity to reach agreement across the boundaries of difference. (p. 14)

Here Bates is drawing on Touraine (2000) regarding the interrelationship between the development of the self and others through communication. Hence we can ask questions about how we enable the student to develop a sense of the self rather than how do we get them to fit the school or the knowledge regimes; how do we enable the student to develop as a reflexive knowledge user and producer rather than how do we transfer established knowing; how do we develop a commitment to security for all rather than generate dependency on structures; and, how do we enable the varied conditions in which all children experience learning to be respected and supported rather than pathologize the needs of particular types of children? As Touraine (2000) argues, 'a school that is no more than an administrative service is unacceptable' (p. 287), and the challenge of educational leadership is not only to expose this but also to provide the opportunity to work for schools and schooling that both reflect the reali-ties of context but also generate new ideas about practice that is worth understanding, thinking about and working for.

Time for work

An enduring personal memory of teaching in a secondary school is one year having fifteen lessons from Monday morning until Wednesday evening, with form period twice a day and duty on a Tuesday as well. The first non-contact period where I could do some marking and preparation was on a Thursday morning. Within the total of 21 lessons a week I had four Year 9 classes for an hour each, which amounted to some 135 stu-dents (plus exercise books to mark) per week, in addition to Year 7, 8, 10, 11 and A level teaching and marking. This was in the mid 1980s, and as far as I can tell nothing much has changed to alleviate the factory system, or the despair that teachers feel at not actually getting to know students. I have to confess that so far as the Year 9 students were concerned, I didn't know all of them and it took a long time and the cultivation of a pho-tographic memory just to learn their names. In contrast, I worked with my A level groups each day. We knew each other, and this provided the security through which we could create insecurity in how we encountered learning and new ways of being and doing in the world.

If I was in a school today then I would be undergoing remodelling through a combination of moving work I shouldn't be doing (e.g. collating reports, display, and data inputting) to teaching assistants and clerical support, and using ICT to access learning resources. Research shows that piloting and learning from these strategies has made a difference to teachers regarding their overall workload and the mainly positive response to changes in working practice (Thomas *et al.* 2004). There seem to be two main strands to this remodelling: first, a focus on the student and how best to enable learning; and second, a reconstitution of the school workforce through which teachers could be in the minority. The two are not unconnected. The government is talking about the importance of 'personalized learning' and how 'our challenge is to design every aspect of school around the different needs to each child, from assessment to teaching, curriculum to engaging parents in the life of the school' (Clarke 2003, p. 2). Such an approach has the potential to enable the development of student agency and would need to be well supported through not only highly qualified teachers but also well-trained learning and organizational support. A less benign reading of policy trends comes from concerns that remodelling is a means of reducing the cost of education and handling the predicted 'shortfall of 30,000 teachers by 2006' through employing unqualified learning support to teach (Stewart 2003b, p. 6). In a paper entitled: 'Workforce Reform – Blue Skies', originating from within the DfES and seen by the *Times Educational Supplement*, the school of the future is described where the only qualified teacher is the headteacher. Deregulation on staffing would mean that learning could be supported by adults other than teachers who could be 'bought in from agencies and seconded but need not be qualified' (Stewart 2003b, p. 6). If teachers are involved then the report says that they will be 'ruthlessly focused on expert teaching, planning and pupil assessment' (p. 6).

If teachers are a scarce resource, and likely to become even scarcer through this proposal, then do we need to continue to focus on their work? Yes we do. This is not just because the paper and such thinking has been condemned but also because while schools need to be packed with adults these members of the school community need to be working with teachers and students. The paper illuminates how teachers and their work have been made *the* problem in education and so the focus is on eradicating this. However, we need to continue to stress that teachers are not necessarily the problem, and that teaching is not an innate quality but a highly skilled job. Perhaps if we focused on letting teachers teach through investment in learning and organizational support then we might be able to attract more graduates to apply, more trained teachers to come back, more teachers to stay, more learning support to want to train as teachers, and more students might aspire to be teachers.

A politics of practice by teachers will enable their positioning by the state through these developments to be challenged, and the opportunity exists to create a more powerful workforce. An interesting place to begin is with how teachers understand their own agency through the link between time and space:

> Teachers take their time seriously. They experience it as a major constraint on what they are able and expected to achieve in their schools. 'No time', 'not enough time', 'need more time' – these are verbal gauntlets that teachers repeatedly throw in the path of enthusiastic innovators. The relationship of time to the teacher runs still deeper than this. Time is a fundamental dimension through which teachers' work is constructed and interpreted by themselves, their colleagues and those who administer and supervise them. Time for the teacher is not just an objective, oppressive constraint but also a subjectively defined horizon of possibility and limitation. Teachers can take time and make time, just as much as they are likely to see time schedules and time commitments as fixed and immutable. Through the prism of time we can therefore begin to see ways in which teachers construct the nature of their work at the same time as they are constrained by it ... Time structures the work of teaching and is in turn structured through it. Time is therefore more than a minor organizational contingency, inhibiting or facilitating management's attempts to bring about change. Its definition and imposition form part of the very core of teachers' work and of the policies and perceptions of those who administer it. (Hargreaves 1994, p. 95)

We can respond to my anecdote and to Hargreaves' analysis in a range of ways. One reading could be negative, because teachers could be seen as being stuck within the organization of time, in what Bauman (2000, p. 113) characterizes as, 'hardware modernity' based on controlling time in order to control our environment through technology and production. In the factory we can make a direct link between the design of work, the space in which it happens and the outcomes of that work. If learning is structured around 'hardware' time then the time for work is fraught with all the problems identified in various studies. PricewaterhouseCoopers (2001, pp. 1–2) study makes the point that 'teachers and headteachers work more intensive weeks than other comparable managers and professionals', but they go on to say that 'on an annual comparison, teachers work at similar levels to other managers and professionals'. This seems to provide the opportunity to look at the organization of the working week, term and year, and within this to look at the type of work that needs to be done and by whom. However, we need to look deeper than this because comparisons with other workers are made in regard to objective data that does not engage with how work is *experienced* during those 'intensive' weeks and the impact on life in what is being characterized as potentially 'less' intensive time. Intensity is not just about working harder because it is term time, but it is about intensification through which all your life (in and out of the school day, in and outside of term time) is full of work, either in front of you on the table or in your head.

Bauman (2000) talks about changes to work through 'software' time which means a shift to 'light modernity' (p. 118) where all is 'instantaneous' and so 'inconsequential':

> … since all parts of space can be reached in the same time-span (that is in 'no-time'), no part of space is privileged, none has 'special value'. If all parts of space can be reached at any moment, there is no reason to worry about securing the right of access to any. If you know that you can visit a place at any time you wish, there is no urge to visit it often or to spend money on a valid-for-life-ticket. There is even less reason to bear the expenditure of perpetual supervision and management, of laborious and risk-fraught husbandry and cultivation of lands which can be easily reached and as easily abandoned following the shifting interests and 'topical relevances'. (p. 118)

For teachers, the experience of this is being overlaid on top of hardware modernity. They know and understand the challenges of this cultural shift for learning and learners, and how it could be used to render their own practice irrelevant. The school as a space for learning becomes redundant when learning knowledge and know how through ICT knowledge-banks are privileged. Teachers as knowledge workers can become suspect when they either don't or poorly acknowledge this type of learning (even if it is because they don't have the resources or training to access it themselves), and so through their practice they are regarded as not knowing and ironically can be caught in the act by mobile phones with integral cameras. School leadership is a very impoverished means of handling these dilemmas because it is conceptualized through the hardware of the organization and the unity of cultural sameness. The challenge of software time means that such thinking leads to what Bauman (2000, p. 122) describes as 'the managerial equivalent of liposuction', which in the private sector has been labelled as downsizing and in education could be increasingly known as remodelling. Auditing the types of work that is done, stopping certain types of work, offloading work to other types of workers is a short-term strategy, but does not automatically interrelate with the challenges of developing learning in an indeterminate world.

A second and more productive reading of my anecdote and Hargreaves' analysis is that we need to think differently about how time is embedded in teacher identity, and how this has been shaped through structures that may undermine rather than productively challenge that identity. Educational leadership is more fertile terrain. It does not have the ringbinder or the guru, but it does have an approach both to engage in the dilemmas of modernity and to enable the people experiencing it to be involved in working through them. As I have argued, educational institutions still have a place in our software world. These institutions might emerge as very different from what they are today, and if teachers are interested in being a part of this then a politics of practice through knowing and knowledge will enable them to be involved in their own and others' learning. Teachers can take the opportunity to control their work: its purposes, structure and development. Teachers have a place in these transient new times because the social is an inevitable part of experience, and we might just realize that even in a 'culture indifferent to eternity and shunning durability' (Bauman 2000, p. 128) questions of morality, and the power issues underpinning them, stubbornly remain, and how we learn as children and as adults to engage with these matters cannot be deleted by the press of a computer key.

References

Alvesson, M. and Sveningsson, S. (2003) 'The Great Disappearing Act: difficulties in doing "leadership"', *Leadership Quarterly*, 14: 359–81.

Anonymous (2001) 'Specialist Business', letters to the editor, *Guardian*, 4 June.

Bagnall, G. (2002) 'Developing Thinking Skills in School', unpublished assignment, Thinking Skills Fellowship, School of Education, University of Birmingham.

Ball, S. J. (2003a) 'The Teacher's Soul and The Terrors of Performativity', *Journal of Education Policy*, 18.2: 215–28.

Ball, S. J. (2003b) *Class Strategies and the Education Market*, London: Routledge Falmer.

Barnett, K. and McCormick, J. (2003) 'Vision, Relationships and Teacher Motivation: a case study', *Journal of Educational Administration*, 41.1: 55–73.

Bassey, M. (1996) 'We are Specialists at Pursuing the Truth', *Times Educational Supplement*, 22 November.

Bates, R. (2002) 'The Impact of Educational Research: alternative methodologies and conclusions', *Research Papers in Education*, 17.4: 1–6.

Bates, R. (2003) 'Can we live together? The ethics of leadership in the learning community', paper presented to the Annual Conference of the British Educational Leadership, Management and Administration Society, Milton Keynes, October 2003.

Bauman, Z. (2000) *Liquid Modernity*, Cambridge: Polity Press.

Begley, P. T. (2001) 'In Pursuit of Authentic School Leadership Practices', *International Journal of Leadership in Education*, 4.4: 353–65.

Bell, L., Bolam, R. and Cubillo, L. (2003) 'Foul is Fair and Fair is Foul: conducting a systematic review of an aspect of educational leadership and management', in L. Anderson and N. Bennett, (eds), *Developing Educational Leadership*, London: SAGE, pp. 85–103.

Bennett, N. and Anderson, L. (eds) (2003) *Rethinking Educational Leadership*, London: SAGE.

Bennett, N., Wise, C., Woods, P. and Harvey, J. A. (2003) *Distributed Leadership*, Nottingham: NCSL.

Birkett, D. (2001) 'The School We'd Like', *Guardian*, Education section, 5 June.

Blackmore, J. (1999) *Troubling Women*, Buckingham: Open University Press.

Blackmore, J. (2000) 'Big Change Questions: can we create a form of public education that delivers high standards for all students in the emerging knowledge society?', *Journal of Educational Change*, 1.4: 381–7.

Bourdieu, P. (1990) *In Other Words*, Cambridge: Polity Press.

Bourdieu, P. (2000) *Pascalian Meditations*, Cambridge: Polity Press.

Carr, W. (1993) 'What is an Educational Practice?', in M. Hammersley (ed.), *Educational Research: Current Issues Vol. 1*, London: Paul Chapman in association with the Open University, pp. 160–76.

Clarke, C. (2003) speech to the new headteacher's conference at the National College for School Leadership, Nottingham, 13 November, www.dfes.gov.uk

Clemson-Ingram, R. and Fessler, R. (1997) 'Innovative Programs for Teacher Leadership', *Action in Teacher Education*, 19.3: 95–106.

Close, T. (2003) 'How Useful are Existing Typologies in Analysing the Leadership and Management Role of Middle Managers?', unpublished EdD assignment, Module 4 Leadership in Education: Senior and Middle Managers, School of Education, University of Birmingham.

Cochran-Smith, M. and Paris, C.L. (1995) 'Mentor and Mentoring: did Homer have it right?', in J. Smyth (ed.), *Critical Discourses on Teacher Development*, London: Cassell, pp. 181–201.

Colleges of Oxford University (1978) 'Joint Scholarship and Entrance Examination in Modern Studies, C(3) Philosophy, Serial Number 58', in *Oxford University Examination Papers, Admission and Entrance Awards, Modern Studies*. Oxford: Clarendon Press.

Contu, A. and Willmott, H. (2000) 'Comment on Wenger and Yanow. Knowing in practice: a "delicate flower" in the organizational learning field', *Organization* 7.2: 269–76.

Court, M. (2003) *Different Approaches to Sharing School Leadership*, Nottingham: NCSL.

Cox, R. W. (1981) 'Social Forces, States, and World Order: beyond international relations theory', *Millennium*, 10.2: 126–55.

Crowther, F. (1997) 'The William Walker Oration, 1996. Unsung heroes: the leaders in our classrooms', *Journal of Educational Administration*, 36.1: 5–17.

Crowther, F. (2002) 'Big Change Question: is the role of the principal in creating school improvement overrated?' *Journal of Educational Change*, 3.2: 167–73.

Crowther, F., Kaagan, S.S., Ferguson, M. and Hann, L. (2002) *Developing Teacher Leaders*, Thousand Oaks, CA: Corwin Press.

Davies, L. (1995) 'Who Needs Headteachers?', keynote address at the British Educational Management and Administration Society Annual Conference, Oxford University, September 1995.

Dean, P. (2001) 'Blood on the Tracks: an accusation and proposal', *Journal of In-service Education*, 27.3: 491–9.

Delanty, G. (2001) *Challenging Knowledge. The university in the knowledge society*, Buckingham: Society for Research into Higher Education and the Open University Press.

Denzin, N. K. (1989) *Interpretive Biography*, Newbury Park, CA: Sage.

Desforges, C. (2003) 'Evidence-informed Policy and Practice in Teaching and Learning', in L. Anderson and N. Bennett (eds) *Developing Educational Leadership*, London: SAGE.

DfES (2003a) *School Workforce in England* (including pupil:teacher ratios, and pupil:adult ratios), January 2003 (revised), national statistics first release, London: DfES, www.dfes.gov.uk/statistics/DB/SFR/

DfES (2003b) *Time for Standards: reforming the school workforce*, London: DfES.

Dowding, K. (1996) *Power*, Buckingham: Open University Press.

Dunne, J. (2003) 'Arguing for Teaching as a Practice: a reply to Alasdair MacIntyre', *Journal of Philosophy of Education*, 37.2: 353–69.

Ebbutt, D., Robson, R. and Worrall, N. (2000) 'Educational Research Partnership: differences and tensions at the interface between the professional cultures of practitioners in schools and researchers in higher education', *Teacher Development*, 4.3: 319–37.

Erben M. (1993) 'The Problem of Other Lives: social perspectives on written biography', *Sociology*, 27.1: 15–25.

Fielding, M. (1999) 'Radical Collegiality: affirming teaching as an inclusive professional practice', *Australian Educational Researcher*, 26.2: 1–34.

Fielding, M. (2000) 'Education Policy and the Challenge of Living Philosophy', *Journal of Education Policy*, 15.4: 377–81.

Fielding, M. (2001) 'Students as Radical Agents of Change', *Journal of Educational Change*, 2.2: 123–41.

Foster, W. (1989) 'Toward a Critical Practice of Leadership', in J. Smyth (ed.), *Critical Perspectives on Educational Leadership*, London: Falmer Press, pp. 39–62.

Frost, D. and Durrant, J. (2003) 'Teacher Leadership: rationale, strategy and impact', *School Leadership and Management*, 23.2: 173–86.

Furedi, F. (2001) 'An Intellectual Vacuum', *Times Higher Education Supplement*, 5 October: 17.

Gardner, H. (1991) *The Unschooled Mind – how children think and how schools should teach*, New York: Basic Books.

Geijsel, F., Sleegers, P., Leithwood, K. and Jantzi, D. (2003) 'Transformational Leadership Effects on Teachers' Commitment and Effort toward School Reform', *Journal of Educational Administration*, 41.3: 228–56.

Gleick, J. (2003) *Isaac Newton*, London: Fourth Estate.

Glickman, C. D. (2002) 'Commentary, More than a Donation: education with public purpose', *International Journal of Leadership in Education*, 5.4: 373–8.

Goodson, I. (1995) 'Studying the Teacher's Life and Work', in J. Smyth (ed.), *Critical Discourses on Teacher Development*, London: Cassell, pp. 55–64.

Grace, G. (1995) *School Leadership: beyond education management*, London: Falmer Press.

Greenfield, T. and Ribbins, P. (1993) *Greenfield on Educational Administration*, London: Routledge.

Gronn, P. (1996) 'From Transactions to Transformations', *Educational Management and Administration*, 24:1: 7–30.

Gronn, P. (2000) 'Distributed Properties: a new architecture for leadership', *Educational Management and Administration*, 28.3: 317–38.

Gronn, P. (2002) 'Distributed Leadership as a Unit of Analysis', *The Leadership Quarterly*, 13: 423–51.

Gronn, P. (2003a) 'Leadership: who needs it?' *School Leadership and Management*, 23.3: 267–90.

Gronn, P. (2003b) *The New Work of Educational Leaders*, London: SAGE.

Gronn, P. (2003c) 'Distributing and Intensifying School Leadership', in N. Bennett and L. Anderson (eds), *Rethinking Educational Leadership*, London: SAGE, pp. 60–73.

Gronn, P. (2003d) 'Leadership's Place in a Community of Practice', in M. Brundrett, N. Burton and R. Smith (eds), *Leadership in Education*, London: SAGE, pp. 23–35.

Gunter, H. M. (1997) *Rethinking Education: The Consequences of Jurassic Management*, London: Cassell.

Gunter, H. M. (1999) 'An Intellectual History of the Field of Education Management from 1960', unpublished PhD thesis, Keele University.

Gunter, H. M. (2001) *Leaders and Leadership in Education*, London: Paul Chapman.

Gunter, H. M. (2003a) 'Teacher Leadership: prospects and possibilities', in M. Brundrett, N. Burton and R. Smith (eds), *Leadership in Education*, London: SAGE, pp. 118–31.

Gunter, H. M. (2003b) 'Introduction: the challenge of distributed leadership', *School Leadership and Management*, 23.3: 261–5.

Gunter, H. M. (2004) 'Labels and Labelling in the Field of Educational Leadership', *Discourse: studies in the cultural politics of education*, 25.1: 21–42.

Gunter, H. M., Brodie, D., Carter, D., Close, T., Farrar, M., Haynes, S., Henry, J., Hollins, K., Nicholson, L., Nicholson, S. and Walker, G. (2003) 'Talking Leadership', *School Leadership and Management*, 23.3: 291–312.

Gunter, H. M. and Ribbins, P. (2002a) 'Leadership Studies in Education: towards a map of the field', *Educational Management and Administration*, 30.4: 387–416.

Gunter, H. M. and Ribbins, P. (2002b) 'Locating Leadership in Education: studying maps and mapping studies', paper presented to the annual conference of the British Educational Leadership, Management and Administration Society, Aston University, Birmingham, September 2002.

Gunter, H. M. and Ribbins, P. (2002c) 'Challenging Orthodoxy in School Leadership Studies: old maps for new directions,' keynote address at the ESRC-funded seminar series, Challenging the Orthodoxy of School Leadership: towards a new theoretical perspective, University of Warwick, November 2002.

Gunter, H. M. and Ribbins, P. (2003a) 'Challenging Orthodoxy in School Leadership Studies: knowers, knowing and knowledge?', *School Leadership and Management*, 23.2: 129–46.

Gunter, H. M. and Ribbins, P. (2003b) 'The Field of Educational Leadership: studying maps and mapping studies, *British Journal of Educational Studies*, 51.3: 254–81.

Gunter, H. M. and Willmott, R. (2002) 'Biting the Bullet', *Management in Education*, 15.5: 35–7.

Hammersley, M. (2001) 'On "Systematic" Review of Research Literatures: a narrative response to Evans and Benefield', *British Educational Research Journal*, 27.5: 543–54.

Harber, C. and Davies, L. (2003) 'Effective Leadership for War and Peace', in M. Brundrett, N. Burton and R. Smith (eds), *Leadership in Education*, London: SAGE, pp. 132–46.

Hargreaves, A. (1994) *Changing Teachers, Changing Times*, London: Cassell.

Harris, A. (2002) 'Distributed leadership in Schools: leading or misleading?', keynote paper presented to the British Educational Leadership, Management and Administration Society Annual Conference, University of Aston, Birmingham, September 2002.

Harris, A. (2003) 'Teacher Leadership as Distributed Leadership: heresy, fantasy or possibility?', *School Leadership and Management*, 23.3: 313–24.

Harris, A. (2004) 'Distributed Leadership and School Improvement: leading or misleading', *Educational Management Administration and Leadership*, 32.1: 11–24.

Harris, A. and Chapman, C. (2002) *Effective Leadership in Schools Facing Challenging Circumstances*, Nottingham: NCSL.

Harris, A. and Lambert, L. (2003) *Building Leadership Capacity for School Improvement*, Maidenhead: Open University Press.

Harris, A. and Muijs, D. (2002) *Teacher Leadership: a review of research*, London: GTC.

Hayes, D. and Butterworth, S. (2001) 'Teacher Activism in Primary Schools in England', *Teacher Development*, 5.3: 357–69.

Helsby, G. (1999) *Changing Teachers' Work*, Buckingham: Open University Press.

Hewitt, B. and Fitzsimons, C. (2001) 'I Quit', *The Guardian Education*, 9 January: 2–3.

Heywood, A. (2000) *Key Concepts in Politics*, Basingstoke: Palgrave.

Hodgkinson, C. (1996) *Administrative Philosophy*, Oxford: Pergamon/ Elsevier Science.

Hogan, P. (2003) 'Teaching and Learning as a Way of Life', *Journal of Philosophy of Education*, 37.2: 207–23.

Hoggart, S. (2001) 'Labour Speak is Easily Learned', *Guardian*, 26 October.

Holland, D. and Lave, J. (2001) 'History in Person, an Introduction', in D. Holland and J. Lave (eds), *History in Person*, Santa Fe, NM: School of American Research Press, pp. 3–33.

Hopkins, D. (2001) *The Think-Tank Report to Governing Council*, Nottingham: NCSL.

Horne, M. (2001) 'Teacher Knows Best', *Guardian*, 4 September.

Hoyle, E. (1982) 'Micropolitics of Educational Organizations', *Educational Management and Administration*, 10.2: 87–98.

Hughes, M. (1985) 'Leadership in Professionally Staffed Organizations', in M. Hughes, P. Ribbins and H. Thomas, *Managing Education: The*

Sytem and The Institution, Eastbourne: Holt, Rinehart and Winston, pp. 262–90.

Jackson, D. (2003) 'Foreword', in A. Harris, and L. Lambert (2003), *Building Leadership Capacity for School Improvement*, Maidenhead: Open University Press, p. x–xxviii.

Jermier, J. M. and Kerr, S. (1997) '"Substitutes for Leadership: their meaning and measurement" – contextual recollections and current observations', *Leadership Quarterly*, 8.2: 95–101.

Jones, K. (2004) 'Teacher Activism? A response to Judith Sachs', *Research Intelligence*, 86 (February): 21–2.

Kaminsky, J. S. (2000) 'The Pragmatic Educational Administrator: "local theory", schooling, and postmodernism reviled', *International Journal of Leadership in Education*, 3.3: 201–24.

Katzenmeyer, M. and Moller, G. (2001) *Awakening the Sleeping Giant: helping teachers develop as leaders*, Thousand Oaks, CA: Corwin Press.

Kirsz, A. (2002) 'An Enquiry into the Effectiveness of a Geography Department in a South Birmingham Boy's Comprehensive School', unpublished EdD assignment, Module 2, Leadership Effectiveness and Improving Schools, School of Education, University of Birmingham.

Lakomski, G. (2002) 'Distributed Leadership: an idea whose time has come?', keynote address at the British Educational Leadership, Management and Administration Society Annual Conference, Aston University, September 2002.

Lave, J. and Wenger, E. (1991) *Situated Learning*, Cambridge: Cambridge University Press.

Leitch, R. and Day, C. (2001) 'Reflective Processes in Action: mapping personal and professional contexts for learning and change', *Journal of In-Service Education*, 27.2: 237–59.

Leithwood, K. (2003) 'Teacher Leadership: its nature, development, and impact on schools and students', in M. Brundrett, N. Burton and R. Smith (eds), *Leadership in Education*, London: SAGE, pp. 103–17.

Leithwood, K. and Jantzi, D. (1999) 'The Relative Effects of Principal and Teacher Sources of Leadership on Student Engagement with School', *Educational Administration Quarterly*, 35 (Supplemental December): 679–706.

Leithwood, K. and Jantzi, D. (2000) 'Principal and Teacher Leadership Effects: a replication', *School Leadership and Management*, 20.4: 415–34.

Leithwood, K., Jantzi, D. and Steinbach, R. (1999), *Changing Leadership for Changing Times*, Buckingham: OUP.

Leithwood, K., Jantzi, D. and Steinbach, R. (2003) 'Fostering Teacher Leadership', in N. Bennett, M. Crawford and M. Cartwright (eds) (2003), *Effective Educational Leadership*, London: Paul Chapman, pp. 186–200.

Lingard, B., Hayes, D., Mills, M. and Christie, P. (2003) *Leading Learning*, Maidenhead: Open University Press.

MacBeath, J. (ed.) (1998) *Effective School Leadership: responding to change*, London: Paul Chapman.

Marks, H. M. and Louis, K.S. (1999) 'Teacher Empowerment and the Capacity for Organizational Learning', *Educational Administration Quarterly*, 35 (supplemental December): 707–50.

McGuinness, C. (1999) *From Thinking Skills to Thinking Classrooms: a review and evaluation of approaches for developing pupil's thinking*, London: Department for Education and Employment.

Muijs, D. and Harris, A. (2003) 'Teacher Leadership – Improvement through Empowerment? An overview of the literature', *Educational Management and Administration*, 31.4: 437–48.

Noddings, N. (2003) 'Is Teaching a Practice?', *Journal of Philosophy of Education*, 37.2: 241–51.

O'Neill, J. (2003) 'Understanding Curriculum Leadership in the Secondary School', in N. Bennett and L. Anderson (eds), *Rethinking Educational Leadership*, London: SAGE.

Ovando, M. N. (1996) 'Teacher Leadership: opportunities and challenges', *Planning and Changing*, 27.1/2: 30–44.

Ozga, J. (1995) 'Deskilling a Profession: professionalism, deprofessionalisation and the new managerialism', in H. Busher and R. Saran (eds), *Managing Teachers as Professionals in Schools*, London: Kogan Page. pp. 21–37.

Ozga, J. (2000a) *Policy Research in Educational Settings*, Buckingham: Open University Press.

Ozga, J. (2000b) 'Leadership in Education: the problem, not the solution?', *Discourse: studies in the cultural politics of education*, 21.3: 355–61.

Polkinghorne, D. E. (1995) 'Narrative Configuration in Qualitative Analysis', in J. Amos Hatch and R. Wisniewski (eds), *Life History and Narrative*, London: Falmer Press.

PricewaterhouseCoopers (2001) *Teacher Workload Study*, London: DfES.

Ranson, S. (1998) 'The Future of Educational Research: learning at the centre', in J. Rudduck and D. McIntyre (eds), *Challenges for Educational Research*, London: Paul Chapman.

Ranson, S. (2000) 'Recognizing the Pedagogy of Voice in a Learning

Community', *Educational Management and Administration*, 28.3: 263–79.

Ranson, S. (2003) 'Public Accountability in the Age of Neo-liberal Governance', *Journal of Education Policy*, 18.5: 459–80.

Rapp, D. (2002) 'Commentary. On lies, secrets, and silence: a plea to educational leaders', *International Journal of Leadership in Education*, 5.2: 175–85.

Reay, D. and Arnot, M. (2004) 'Participation and Control in Learning: a pedagogic democratic right?' in L. Poulson and M. Wallace (eds), *Learning to Read Critically in Teaching and Learning*, London: SAGE, pp. 151–72.

Reay, D. and Ball, S. J. (2000) 'Essentials of Female Management', *Educational Management and Administration*, 35.3: 253–67.

Reid, A. (2002) 'Public Education and Democracy: a changing relationship in a globalizing world', *Journal of Education Policy*, 17.5: 571–85.

Ribbins, P., Bates, R. and Gunter, H. M. (2003) 'Reviewing Research in Education in Australia and the UK: evaluating the evaluations', *Journal of Educational Administration*, 41.4: 423–44.

Ribbins, P. and Gunter, H. M. (2002) 'Mapping Leadership Studies in Education: towards a typology of knowledge domains', *Educational Management and Administration*, 30.4: 359–86.

Ribbons, P. and Gunter, H. M. (2003) 'Leadership Studies in Education: Maps for EPPI Reviews' in L. Anderson and N. Bennett (eds), *Developing Educational Leadership*, London: SAGE, pp. 168–184.

Ribbins, P. and Zhang, J. (2003) 'Art and Artistry in the Theory and Practice of Educational Administration', *The Practising Administrator, Monograph 33*, 25.4: 1–16.

Rollins, M.-T. (2002) 'Learning to be Independent: research into improvement of homework completion rate', unpublished school-based action-research project for Management for Learning, School of Education, University of Birmingham.

Sachs, J. (2000) 'The Activist Professional', *Journal of Educational Change*, 1.1: 77–95.

Sennett, R. (1999) *The Corrosion of Character*, New York: Norton.

Sennett, R. (2002) *The Fall of Public Man*, London: Penguin.

Sergiovanni, T. J. (2001) *Leadership: what's in it for schools?*, London: RoutledgeFalmer.

Sikes, P. (1997) *Parents who Teach*, London: Cassell.

Sikes, P. (2001) 'Teachers' Lives and Teaching Performance', in D. Gleeson and C. Husbands (eds), *The Performing School*, London: RoutledgeFalmer, pp. 86–100.

Silins, H. and Mulford, B. (2002) 'Schools as Learning Organisations: the case for system, teacher and student learning', *Journal of Educational Administration*, 40.5: 425–46.

Smith, P. (1997) 'Tyranny of the Thought Police', *Times Education Supplement Extra: Social Sciences*, 21 February: 1.

Smith, S. (2001) 'Multiple Intelligences at case study Technology College', unpublished action-research project, School of Education, University of Birmingham.

Smylie, M. A. and Brownlee-Conyers, J. (1992) 'Teacher Leaders and their Principals: exploring the development of new working relationships', *Educational Administration Quarterly*, 28.2: 150–84.

Smyth, J. (2001) *Critical Politics of Teachers' Work*, New York: Peter Lang.

Spillane, J. P., Coldren, A. and Diamond, J. B. (2001) *Elementary School Leadership: the development and distribution of knowledge for and about instruction*, presented to the annual meeting of the American Educational Research Association, Seattle, April.

Spillane, J. P., Diamond, J. B. and Jita, L. (2003) 'Leading Instruction: the distribution of leadership for instruction', *Journal of Curriculum Studies*, 35.5: 533–43.

Spillane, J. P., Halverson, R. and Diamond, J. B. (2004) 'Toward a Theory of Leadership Practice: a distributed perspective', *Journal of Curriculum Studies*, in press.

Starratt, R. J. (2003) *Centering Educational Administration*, Mahwah, NJ: Lawrence Erlbaum Associates.

Stewart, W. (2003a) 'Staff Cuts Running into Thousands', *Times Educational Supplement*, 29 August.

Stewart, W. (2003b) 'Storm out of Blue Skies', *Times Educational Supplement*, 5 December.

Teacher Training Agency (2003) *Qualifying to Teach: professional standards for Qualified Teacher Status and requirements for Initial Teacher Training*, London: TTA, www.tta.gov.uk/training/qtsstandards/

Thomas, H., Brown, C., Butt, G., Fielding, A., Foster, J., Gunter, H., Lance, A., Potts, E., Powers, S., Rayner, S., Rutherford, D., Selwood, I. and Szwed, C. (2003) 'Moderning the School Workforce: developing perspectives', paper presented to the British Educational Research Association, Heriot-Watt University, September 2003.

Thomas, H., Butt, G., Fielding, A., Foster, J., Gunter, H., Lance, A., Potts, E., Powers, S., Rayner, S., Rutherford, D., Selwood, I. and Szwed, C. (2004) *Transforming the School Workforce: Pathfinder project research brief*, London: DfES.

Thrupp, M. and Willmott, R. (2003) *Education Management in Managerialist Times*, Maidenhead: Open University Press.

Touraine, A. (2000) *Can we Live Together?*, Stanford, CA: Stanford University Press.

Wallace, M. (2001) 'Sharing Leadership of Schools through Teamwork: a justifiable risk?', *Educational Management and Administration*, 29.2: 153–67.

Watkins, C. and Mortimore, P. (1999) 'Pedagogy: what do we know?', in P. Mortimore (ed.), *Understanding Pedagogy and its Impact on Learning*, London: Paul Chapman.

Wenger, E. (1998) *Communities of Practice*, Cambridge: Cambridge University Press.

Wenger, E. (2000) 'Communities of Practice and Social Learning Systems', *Organization*, 7.2: 225–46.

Wenger, E. and Snyder, W. (2000) 'Communities of Practice: the organizational frontier', *Harvard Business Review*, January–February: 139–45.

Winch, C. and Foreman-Peck, L. (2000) 'Teacher Professionalism, Educational Aims and Action Research: the evolution of policy in the United Kingdom', *Teacher Development*, 4.2: 165–76.

Winkley, D., with Pascal, C. (1998) 'Developing a Radical Agenda', in C. Pascal and P. Ribbins (eds), *Understanding Primary Headteachers*, London: Cassell.

Winter, R. (1991) 'Post-modern Sociology as a Democratic Educational Practice? Some suggestions', *British Journal of Sociology of Education*, 12.4: 467–81.

Woods, P. A. (2004) 'Democratic Leadership: drawing distinctions with distributed leadership', *International Journal of Leadership in Education: Theory and Practice*, 7.1: 3–26.

Woodward, W. (2003) 'A Third of Teachers Plan to Quit', *Guardian*, 7 July.

Index